D0616944

THE ART OF STILLNESS IN A NOISY WORLD

Magnus Fridh

Translated by Ian Giles

Hardie Grant
BOOKS

First published by © Bonnier Fakta 2019
This edition published in 2020 by Hardie Grant Books,
an imprint of Hardie Grant Publishing

Hardie Grant Books (London)
5th & 6th Floors
52–54 Southwark Street
London SE1 1UN

Hardie Grant Books (Melbourne)
Building 1, 658 Church Street
Richmond, Victoria 3121

hardiegrantbooks.com

British Library Cataloguing-in-Publication Data. A catalogue record for this book is available from the British Library.

The Art of Stillness in a Noisy World
ISBN: 978-1-78488-369-0
10 9 8 7 6 5 4 3 2 1

For the Swedish edition:
Design and illustrations: Kristin Lidström
Editor: Anna Sodini

For the English edition:
Publishing Director: Kate Pollard
Editorial Assistant: Alexandra Lidgerwood
Translator: Ian Giles
Typesetter: David Meikle
Proofreader: Sarah Herman

Colour reproduction by p2d
Printed and bound in China by Leo Paper Products Ltd.

5

Preface

SOMETIMES JUST TO sit in silence and do nothing is one of the wisest things a person can do in these times in which we live. I mean being truly still and silent with both body and mind. It may be more necessary than ever, but it is hardly something new. As early as the 17th century, Blaise Pascal, the French mathematician and philosopher, wrote in his collection *Thoughts*: 'All of humanity's problems stem from man's inability to sit quietly in a room alone.' Perhaps this is a fundamental need that we are not always capable of meeting but of which we constantly need to remind ourselves. When life is going the way we want it to, it is quite easy to forget, but when we are faced with a calendar clogged with borderline impossible demands, it seems as if the space to do nothing has disappeared.

In my daily life, there are three specific instances when I am noticeably more still and am thus able to experience a direct positive effect from being still in itself.

The first instance is a do-nothing activity I often engage in when I get home from work. I like to sit down and spend five to 10 minutes with our cat. It's become a pleasant routine and as soon as I sit down on our sofa, she comes to lie next to me. Her tempo is different, calmer. This is incredibly infectious and I soon find that my own movements become slower, softer and more compliant. My body absorbs her rhythm, and when I spend time with her I do nothing else but sit with her. My phone is left out of reach and I can feel how tensions and sharp edges are softened during that time. In a moment of unplanned rest without a defined end time, a door is pushed open a little way to something that is more still. A bit like coming inside from the more urgent and pressing outside world to a no-man's land – further into a calmer existence. From on to off. From doing to being. From connected to disconnected.

The second instance is when I am outdoors, in the natural world. In nature, you can freely bypass yourself and become more observant. There arises an interface between yourself and nature, and the familiar feeling of participation often emerges. Your senses can then be fully awakened, you can once again be grounded, and in contrast to the urban environment it is easier to unwind from the chaos of daily life. In this nuanced reunion, stress is reduced, blood pressure is lowered and mood and creativity are improved. These appear to be the effects of what we refer to as *forest bathing*. A rising sense of abode.

I live in the middle of a big city. In the middle of the courtyard that our apartment block surrounds there is a tree – a magnificent maple that extends to the windowsill on the fourth floor where we live. In an environment that is nothing but asphalt, this tree has a special meaning. I notice it on a daily basis and appreciate it. The changing seasons calm me, as well as the knowledge that everything is transient. Although it may sound sentimental to say so, transience is quite natural when you understand that you should be compliant with its rhythm. The magic of the ordinary passing of time.

The third instance is during my daily meditation. This is a time that is as still as possible. Almost powerfully still. Both in the outer form and the inner.

After a long day, the sensation of activity sometimes lingers on and can shift from one body part to another like an itch. It eventually dissipates, and the body stops hurrying, seeming to find solace in being still. Within me, the noise is markedly reduced; after a while activity is almost completely minimised, and I tap into a permissive and pleasant emptiness. Regardless of mood or circumstance, some days when I meditate, I experience a happiness that knows no bounds. In the midst of daily life. In the midst of stress. In the midst of everything hurrying on. When it appears, I don't seek to change anything in particular – I lower my guard, and the boundary between myself and others seems to become increasingly abstract.

The common effect of these three instances is the fundamental recovery and replenishment of energy that I experience in the stillness and the silence. On more than one occasion, I have felt the outer limit of brutal fatigue which can make even the simplest of decisions seem difficult. Too tired to think, too empty to feel – the daily moments of stillness are a countermeasure that provide a deep and lingering calm. But it's not only that. How can we ever know who we are if we never completely stop and fall silent? How are we even supposed to be able to hear our own thoughts?

At the time of writing, the Swedish Work Environment Authority reports that poor health is on the rise in Sweden's workplaces, with chronic fatigue syndrome one of the prevalent outcomes. There are a total of 1.4 million people in Sweden's workplaces suffering from work-related issues. Half of them report feeling anxious or worried or suffering from sleep disorders. One cause that is mentioned in this context is that the boundary between work and private life has been erased. I see myself in this and recognise how easy it is to be unable to draw a line between the two, as well as how important it has become to create clear areas for recovery in the life I live. How can we find that in our daily lives? How do we find the micro-moments that restore energy and motivation? In a series of standalone thoughts that use meditative exercises as their building blocks throughout, I will share some reflections on what it is that enables me, in the life I live, to be still in a noisy world.

I.

Daily Life

13

Finding Stillness

FINDING YOUR SILENCE and stillness is the theme throughout this book. Experiencing the space in life that creates clarity and meaning instead of being controlled by stress and always being in an inescapable, hectic rush. That's really all that it is about, and I think I can help you to find it.

Stillness can be found in many different places, under different names, and under different circumstances. For some, it can be found in the wind across the land, while for others it is experienced more clearly in the white noise of city hubbub. It can be found in the pauses of language, while also being found in the deep listening to those sounds that break the silence.

Meditation offers some particularly well-honed techniques that make it more possible to notice stillness. It's important to maintain it, so that it becomes part of your daily life.

The method can even help to quieten down your thoughts and enable healthy responses to stress. Try out the different exercises that are featured throughout the book. Let the act of reading itself be meditative – but you can also put the book down for a while, once you have read the exercise instructions, and simply be still.

Meditation cannot solely be studied through books – what really benefits you is direct experience. With a mind constantly moving from one thing to another, between the past and future, discouragement and enthusiasm, you need to have a lot of patience. What is certain is that practise will pay dividends. A number of research reports tell us this. It works for everyone and anyone – including people like me who have innately short concentration spans. Just the other day, I received a message from a woman who had experienced the same thing: 'I'll never forget the first time I tried meditation. My whole body was crawling and I couldn't sit still. After 30 seconds I thought to myself – no way, this isn't for me! I couldn't have been more wrong.'

If your exercises become more regular, not only will your ability to be present be significantly enhanced but you will also eventually experience stillness and silence enveloping you. Not closing in, or excluding or short circuiting. *Enveloping* – what a beautiful word! Something that doesn't last forever but which still creates an invisible protective cover that gently holds you in silence without excluding the outside world. In the same way that fog can envelop an entire landscape. Or that layers of skin envelop your body.

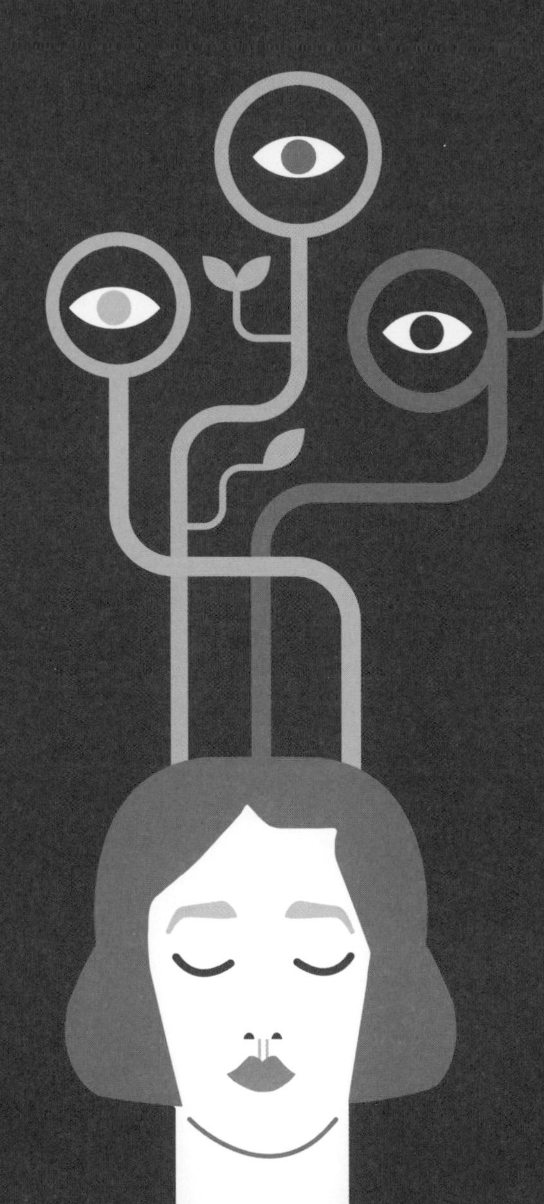

17

Stillness is Everything and Nothing

STILLNESS IS EVERYTHING but at the same time nothing. Undemanding, it is there when we let go of our histories, our fixed principles and our self-absorption. When we touch it, it can sometimes make us experience a sense of where our being is. A feeling that life is for real. A wealth of contentment beyond what we have achieved and our highly focused ambitions. As Stig Dagerman said: 'My life is not a thing that should be measured... A human life is also not a performance, but is growth towards perfection. And that perfection does not perform – it works while at rest.'

You don't become anyone else when meditating. You don't need to change your style of clothing or taste in music, accept any particular faith or travel to distant countries. Instead, you become more like you are. Yourself. I don't really know what the expression *get to know yourself* means, other than being a recurring reflection of life's changes in relation to what seems to be still and gathered within yourself, and the insight that emerges from within. When you can reach beyond the narrowly subjective.

Ever since I was little, my train of thought has always had furious momentum. Fortunately I acquired meditative techniques a long time ago in order to tame my thoughts in their onslaught. Like me, I think there are many who meditate in pursuit of what is steadfastly still. It is an attempt to make contact with the supporting building blocks: A kind of prehistoric element in humankind that is still present in that which grows and in itself creates the meaning of existence. Nothing else has given me more understanding of my own existence than still silence. My experience is that this is attainable and necessary for anyone and everyone. It is there to be found even in the more basic meditation techniques.

For in the same moment that the meditator enters the zone of stillness, heavy becomes light, high flying is grounded, every challenge and hardship is reasonable – and I sometimes feel that I am touched by something that is truly and absolutely radiant. Like love.

The first time I tried meditation, it was as if a calming hand was placed on my shoulder and a voice whispered into my whole body: 'It'll be okay, it's alright and you're good enough.' For a shattered teenager, these words were transformative and I chose to take them with me. Perhaps you also feel a similar need sometimes? A longing to slow down. To feel collected and less exhausted. After the initial steps and a dose of stubborn practise, meditation lays new ground underfoot; it becomes a natural compass and a fundamental need. Like me, I expect you don't have that much time. But perhaps you can find a few gaps in your day when you can withdraw for a few minutes for some time spent in stillness.

Sometimes I think that's all it takes. Being still enough to hear the beat of our own hearts – to understand where we are going and to remind ourselves what is important in our lives.

Place a hand on your ribcage and be present in the rising and falling movement. Each inhalation. Each exhalation.

Absorb the increasing calm without any goal or purpose. Completely, unmovingly still – just a moment longer. For no other reason than being still.

Let it envelop you.

21

The Stillness We Seek

FORTY PEOPLE SIT motionless in a room. It is early on a November morning. The time of day when, for the last 10 years, I have taught yoga and meditation in a suburb of the city in which I live. Less than 10 minutes ago, the room was filled with the loud buzz of voices – friendly, cheerful conversations. Now everyone is sitting on the floor with their legs crossed, hands resting on their knees, eyes shut, voluntarily still and silent. Some quickly find a seated posture that works for them, getting their body to relax, while others move about a little before eventually settling into a comfortable position. It is easy to see how the restlessness lingers on for a while, and it takes a couple of minutes before the silence has entirely come to rest like a thick blanket covering the room.

Time and space disappear with each breath as we move into the domain of simplicity. My instructions go from expansive to pared back in a shared, carefully maintained presence. Together, we share the experience of being free from necessities for that moment. Perhaps we just forget ourselves for a while – is it that simple? Is it a permitted rest from those masks that we wear?

Those of us sitting here together don't really know much about each other. Our roles are completely unimportant in that moment.

Noise becomes silence. Together, we experience how hustle and bustle become clarified calm. Distraction becomes a state of attentiveness. Our inner duality is vanquished in these opposites and contrasts.

There is a clear feeling of recovery in this inward-looking, unassuming gathering, and no matter how strange it may sound, it is clearly visible on the face of the meditator that calmness is spreading through them. The experience becomes the arena for what words can't quite explain. I often think about a verse in the *Katha Upanishad*, written in around the 5th century BC. It is a description of a deep, resting state of a contemporary 'existence and disappearance… Something that can only be understood by saying "it is".'

Outside there is heavy, grey cloud cover. Incipient rain patters irregularly and cautiously on the windowsill. The wind picks up and causes a poorly fixed tarpaulin to flap up and down, making a faint knocking sound as a result. The lights in the room are dimmed and the subdued light provides a soothing backdrop to this introspective pause. Perhaps it is one of the few moments in the week where we are truly still and manage to become conscious of what we actually feel, without quibbling and evaluating its substance. From everything at once to nothing.

An hour later, an undramatic conclusion. Some leave the room in silence. Others stay on, talking quietly for a while.

As the Finland-Swedish poet Gunnar Björling once wrote: 'The stillness we seek, we seek the answer, the answer that has no name, our heart's life, like the stillness we seek... it gives no advice and no harbour, it gives life.'

25

Red Light

GOING UPHILL ON the way to my place of work: The morning creeps in tantalisingly, barely distinguishable from the darkness. The tang of the February wind and the panoply of sounds that are drawn out in my head. My body moves forward far too quickly for comfort, my shoulders pulled up towards my ears.

A minute or so later I reach a pedestrian crossing together with several others, just as it signals to stop.

Some of them, more practised than others, hurry across the street through the diesel fumes before the revving cars can zoom off on green. One person stands one step into the road, almost as if he is on the starting blocks for the next round. It is as if he is in motion, even though he is waiting. He rocks restlessly back and forth.

Another takes his phone from his coat pocket, bows his head and occupies himself for the present. Although somewhere else.

I have hurried like this many times before, but on this particular day I take note of its significance and stop completely.

On this particular morning, it feels like my internal

battery is running low. The cogs in my brain need to rest. I can feel it clearly. It has been like that a lot recently.

I remain standing a little way back on the kerb as vehicles rush past, completely still, with my arms hanging passively at my sides. My empty hands are open and I happen to think that it might look a bit odd. A second later this sudden idea is explained when I realise I am the only living being as far as the eye can see who is standing completely still.

The traffic light has awakened something suddenly – an intuitive presence. I feel the weight of my body. It is as if my feet are rooted in the asphalt. I spread my toes, pressing them towards the ground. My weight is evenly distributed, the foundations calibrate the misplaced mobilisation of energy and a boundary is closed to the urgency. I lift my gaze and on the other side of the street I see twinkling sunlight reflected in a third-floor window. The red seconds that normally seem so long become a pleasant feeling of returning to what I call the origin level. What you feel when the pieces of the jigsaw fall back into their right places again. Some people refer to it as: *When you stop being just in your head.*

The red colour of the traffic light has become like the bell that regularly chimes at the monastery of the Vietnamese Buddhist monk Thich Nhat Hanh in southern France. Several times a day, those staying there hear the given signal for awakening their presence. In the same moment, everyone stops whatever they are doing. The presence bell summons them and those who stop know to relax their body and focus on their breathing. The signal restores calm and a sense of freedom. Perhaps I have found my own presence signal at a pedestrian crossing in the middle of the big city.

As I stand there, quite still, my attention is drawn to a movement: My inhalation and exhalation in a simple breathing technique that offers a positive, calming effect. I breathe in while calmly counting to four, breathe out and once again count to four. Once all the air is emptied out, I rest in the interval before the next inhalation lasting another four seconds.

I follow the air from the opening of the nostrils, and then with precision as it moves in and out of my body. I watch how I am affected by the presence of the breathing. How all the tensions in my body gradually give way and how my perspective can change within an incredibly short period of time.

Perhaps it is too great a word to use about an ordinary day while waiting for a red light to change colour, but I suddenly feel free. Free from the hustle and bustle.

After a few cycles of breathing in and out, I see the reflection of the green light in a puddle. One minute has elapsed. One minute to win or lose.

I walk on, step by step, in the same direction as before. My shoulders have relaxed completely. The urge for speed has left me and I have found my pace. There is a marvellous silence in my body and I feel the breath fill my lungs from the bottom up.

It can be a liberation to stop at a red light.

Life is getting out

31

Life is Getting Out

IN THE PAST, there would be a yellow, rectangular metal plaque with the inscription *Danger to life when leaning out* attached to the bottom of windows on trains. In my teens, I saw that sign where someone had crossed through eight of the letters and given the first 'a' an umlaut. Suddenly, a new sentence was created with a completely different, multifaceted meaning: *Life is getting out*. I was fascinated by the inventiveness of the scribbler; for the young punk rocker I was back then, this new message had hopeful associations: *Get out of society's hamster wheel, get out of what is established and stagnant. Get out and change.*

Recently I happened to see, by chance, a picture of that amended metal plaque. The one-liner still appealed to me just as much. It still delivered the same associations, although with some modification: *Get away from society's elevated stress levels, get away from the demands more and more people experience these days, get out and gain time to recover. Get out and feel free.*

Once upon a time, long ago, there lived a young prince in Nepal by the name of Siddharta Gotama. He was raised in total luxury, and because of his parents' overprotection, he was shielded from life outside the family's palace. But one day in adulthood, his curiosity got the better of him and he escaped from the palace. Outside of the palace walls, he met an old person and realised that we all change. He met a sick person and realised that we all suffer . He saw a dead person and realised that everything is temporary and will eventually perish. Siddharta wanted to go out into the world and understand what the meaning of all this could be. After years of searching, he eventually stopped – as still and imperturbable as a mountain in his meditation, which led him to a realisation that still resonates in our modern times. He referred to the way out as *Nirvana*. According to the new Buddha, Nirvana wasn't something to wait for in a future life. Nirvana exists right here in the quality of every moment, in the direct ability to accept and fully embrace life's circumstances if we apply the right attentiveness in our minds and bodies. The only way out was in.

According to the Buddha, being still was the ability to carefully balance attention and relaxation. The middle way is the way that provides resonance and sound.

My own way out from stress and anxiety has for a long time been to first relax and then make myself stop struggling in matters over which I have no control so that I can better focus on what I have the ability to influence. Call it acknowledgement or acceptance. It has shifted my perspective on most things in my existence – it has worked during tough trials.

Every time I hear Reinhold Nieburh's words 'God, grant me the serenity to accept the things I cannot change, the courage to change the things I can, and the wisdom to know the difference,' I think that those lines explain what acceptance with wisdom involves better than anything else. In that kind of soil, it is possible for both gratitude and compassion to take root.

A special relaxation exercise has worked during difficult times and laid good foundations for continued meditation. It adds depth to basic breathing, it releases tension and it opens the first door to the experience of stillness.

It isn't always easy for an overloaded mind to relax, but through micro-adjustments to specific areas of the body you can take steps to find your way there. My experience is that a couple of specific body parts, three anchor points, contribute to an effortless feeling of wholeness.

And they are the small muscles in our faces that we use without even thinking about it! It becomes clear that they have been especially active when we passivise them, and the first anchor point is the muscles around and behind our eyes.

First you let the skin on your face 'hang' slightly.

Just as if all the muscles you have used during the day for articulation, smiling and expressions now get to rest for a while. Your cheeks become slack, almost as if a compassionate hand is gently stroking your face.

Your forehead is smooth and wide as your eyebrows sink down slightly, and the gap between your eyebrows is kept relaxed.

You can look up and keep your eyes still for a couple of seconds. Then look down, and finally extend your gaze to the sides in the same way. Then let the muscles around your eyes relax. You don't need to close your eyes completely, but let your eyelids grow heavy and keep your eye muscles relaxed. Perhaps it may feel good to cup your hands over your eyes until you feel your eyes relaxing a little, or massage the area around your eyebrows with the tips of your thumbs in gentle circular motions.

When you exhale, you will feel a connection to the area behind the eye itself. The eye is allowed to rest after all the impressions it has absorbed during the day. Assume, for the time being, that you can no longer influence anything positively or negatively. Let things be – for now, there is nothing important to see.

Then, the second anchor point. Move the feeling of presence into your mouth and note the position and activity of your tongue. First, press the tip of your tongue against the roof of your mouth, then stop. Let your tongue sink down to rest, and let the back of your tongue spread wide across your mouth. Experience your palate and your jaw relaxing. Imagine that your tongue is falling silent as all words leave it. Everything that wants to become language and wants to be expressed in the moment remains unsaid.

Direct your attention to your stomach. Tighten your abdomen for a couple of seconds and then pull it in deeply towards your spine before releasing it. Track with precision how your stomach rises and falls with each inhalation and exhalation. Experience your ponderings, worries and deep tensions slowly leaving your body.

Eyes, tongue, stomach at rest. Experience your whole body in a state of deep relaxation. Micro-adjust and encourage your mind to silence.

Feel how you slowly and comfortably make your way out of what made you tense and stressed. Out of what has held you in its grip. Get out.

37

The Art of Doing Nothing

La dolce far niente is the phrase Italians use to describe time in which you enjoy doing nothing. There is no equivalent expression in English. On the other hand, the need for breaks seems to be greater than ever; regardless of how strange it may sound, in our daily lives we find it hard to allow ourselves to be still, to treat ourselves to it and above all to see its benefits.

It sometimes feels as if we want to apologise when we have phased out of action, despite the fact that we spend much of our waking hours engaged in action. Even lying still on the sofa and watching television or scrolling through a stream of social media feed are things that I consider doing in this context. Connected, accessible and always available.

Doing nothing is something else. Deep down we can feel that we need it. During weary moments in daily life we long for it: A break from everything. Nevertheless, it requires a certain degree of effort to achieve. Recently, I bumped into an acquaintance in the street who replied to my 'How are things?' question as follows: 'I'm tired right down to my bones.' I understand what that means, and it isn't just a case of stopping – we're far too used to the opposite: Ambition, big plans. But phasing out and doing the minimum is nothing but a gift to ourselves. Finding your own places and opportunities to experience silence and stillness. Stress is already suppressed after a couple of deep breaths, and melts away like ice turning to water. Your beam of focus is re-positioned in the right place to cast its light on what is important in your life. Your life blood.

Being must constitute the basic foundation of doing. I now find this arrangement different and far more advantageous in the daily life I lead. A micro-pause or other breathing space like this can be as brief as five or 15 minutes. You can lie down or sit up on your sofa or bed. The main thing is that the place you choose is a calm place with as little distraction as possible. Put your phone and computer well away from yourself. Switch off all notifications and alarms.

Now get ready to do nothing. Get ready to be pleasantly idle.

Take a few slow, deep breaths through your nose. Feel the breaths wash through your entire body like a relaxing massage around the abdomen, ribs and shoulder blades. Let your breathing become pleasantly calm. Release your tension and unnecessary thoughts.

Let your attention be capacious and discover how light your concentration can be. Your body can be completely relaxed, but you are actively awake in your experience of the movement of your breathing. Now take a couple of minutes to move your presence to your brow. Perhaps you can sense the presence as a tingling, an increasing relaxation or as a light warmth. Keep the presence focused on the sensations in your forehead for a while, before slowly moving on to the experience in your entire body.

When you are ready to stop, remain still while you open your eyes. Experience how stillness is not just there when you close your eyes, and is not just an inward-looking state – it also remains when you open your eyes. Experience this in a wide awake state.

Experience your body in stillness. Experience your mind in stillness. In silence. Still.

In his work *On the Shortness of Life*, the philosopher Seneca wrote: 'The part of life we really live is small.' For me, being still belongs to this part, and this is incredibly clear during those pauses. And when you experience this more deeply, gratitude feels like the only suitable reaction.

41

Silence in Compassion

MY FAMILY IS gathered in a close circle, sitting on a thick, wine-red carpet in a room in Shechen Monastery in a suburb of Nepal's capital, Kathmandu. Around us are all the Buddhist symbols you can think of and it is clear from the iconography which former teachers developed the monastic traditions leading up to the present day. The importance of history is evident in the careful reverence.

Also part of our circle is Tulku Jigmey Samten, a friend who is a member of the small group of *special* Buddhist teachers who were identified by monastic scholars early in life. They gave him the title *Tulku*. He explains that since childhood he had wanted to live in a monastery and had been deeply disappointed when his parents decided that ordinary schooling would be more appropriate. After his basic education, the choice was easy: He has lived for many years together with 400 monks in a monastery that is in no way isolated from the outside world. During the day, the distant rumble of traffic is audible as cars career along roads that are often just tracks. At night, the neighbourhood dogs bark in an agitated call and response that only dies down when day returns. They have kept me awake for many nights, and I have become aware of their inverted circadian rhythm after seeing several of them now sleeping heavily in a row outside the walls of the monastery.

Jigmey replies calmly to the question posed by my daughters about whether he experiences stress. 'Of course! We experience stress and negative emotions too. It's completely natural.'

There is even distraction in the monastery, and many of the monks have their own mobile phones – 'the miracle of our time' as Jigmey calls them. The monastery elders have advocated that one should be permitted to have 'old, black-and-white telephones' without all the modern features. This proposal was rejected, given that many monks want to be accessible via ubiquitous media such as WeChat, Facebook and YouTube. Several of the monks regularly stretch the current monastic rules, and a mobile can easily be concealed in a monk's habit and brought into the classroom. 'Smartphones make us servants,' says Jigmey. 'I'm curious about new electronics and impressed by them, but sometimes I honestly just feel like throwing away my phone.' While Jigmey shows us around and tells us about one of the beautiful statues in the room – Avalokiteshvara – the depiction of our own inner compassion, I glance out through the fine mesh of the wire mosquito net. Outside I see one of the younger monks dribbling a ball through a somewhat rickety defence. He dispatches a steady shot towards the bottom left-hand corner of the temporary goal. Close to the post. Yes! A brief cheer and the wine-red fabric of the goalscorer's habit flutters in the low sunshine as he pirouettes in a gesture of celebration, stretching his right arm up. The happiness is there in that moment. We live beneath the same sun, we experience the same joy, we have the same obstacles to overcome and we have the same desire for context and meaning. But there is a difference here, and we continue to listen attentively to Jigmey: 'In order to deal with anxiety, worry and stress when it hits us, you have to practise and prepare by having some motivation that you want to return to again and again. The motivation we use here in the monastery is based on wishing others well. It might be brief rituals that I perform every morning and night that provide calm.' Meditation on compassion in the Buddhist context is a foundation that forms the basis for all meditation. A compassion that is characterised by wisdom, in the sense that we cultivate an understanding of why suffering happens and how we can realistically handle certain situations. Compassion becomes a catalyst for acting according to the best of our ability, but it also allows us to understand that we should accept our limitations and not worry about what we cannot influence in the moment.

Jigmey continues: ‘In short, you motivate yourself using your mind and steering it in a positive direction. The method is based on reflecting on good wishes for others and yourself. Quite simply, you wish others well intentionally. Try it. Try doing it twice a day, for about five minutes each time.’

Connecting to stillness; being prepared. Training your mind just as many of us spend time honing a fit body. The Buddhist method places a great deal of emphasis on actively training oneself in compassion. During the day, it is the monk’s natural duty to colour every action with thoughts of good. Every morning, every hour, every breath is a new opportunity. This permeates through and takes shape in daily life.

'If you do these exercises regularly, you gain a new structure that at some time in your life will be of great use. It makes life simpler. You feel better, others feel better and negative feelings seem more manageable,' Jigmey continues as we go outside into the chilly evening air.

A monk passes us by, his head lowered in walking meditation. A few metres away there is a small gaggle of monks who don't notice our presence even for a moment. They are gathered around an older monk. He is holding something in his hand. In the dim light, the screen of the mobile phone illuminates their faces as if they were looking straight down at a glittering treasure.

The darkness lays its densely woven blanket atop the monastery and we use our iPhones to find our way back to our temporary accommodation. A four-legged mongrel passes silently by my leg and I recoil. A minute or so later the first bark echoes into the dusk. An immediate reply is heard from a distance. And I was hoping to sleep well tonight.

47

Mindfulness in Daily Life

MINDFULNESS IS ABOUT cultivating the ability to be intentionally focused on presence. And I think that looking at life as a series of moments can lend a new perspective. Each one of them contains an inherent meaning. The automatic and habitual are replaced with an experience of reality. It is a clear and unadulterated alertness that not only creates nuance but also a feeling of being lifted out of your own first-person experience.

It's the month of July in the county of Blekinge in southern Sweden. One day after another passes by at a stately pace, Mediterranean style. On the blue globe thistles in front of the porch steps of our summer house bumblebees buzz to and fro at a brisk tempo. It is impossible to tell how many of them there are. Our front door is wide open and all the sounds of the garden make their way into the main room.

I'm doing the dishes when it suddenly hits me that you can wash up in several different ways. You can choose to do the dishes as if it's something you want to get out of the way quickly so that you can rush on to the next activity. Or in a household, it could be seen as an enduring measure of fairness if the person doing the dishes knows with absolute certainty whether or not it is his or her turn. You can also perform the washing up with a negative attitude if you consider it to be a pointless, time-wasting activity – a means to an end.

Another, more interesting way of doing the dishes is to do so attentively. This can take shape from something as banal as listening to the sound of the water filling the sink, smelling the scent of the washing-up liquid or feeling the temperature of the water against your skin. Granted, it's a somewhat peculiar way to do the dishes, but it has none of the negativity and it is the opposite of the rushing moment in which part of the time at our disposal vanishes and is lost.

By rushing, you are already in the future, in your past, or simply in the shadows of existence.

Inspired by the Zen monk's description – how something as simple as drinking a cup of tea with the right presence drives away his loneliness – and a study in which people who carried out a daily activity with the right intention and awareness lowered their levels of stress and anxiety by 27 per cent, I am empowered in exploration of the everyday.

After taking on the job of dishwasher more or less daily during our weeks of holiday, I noticed a growing calm as I focused more and more on the precise details of doing the washing up. I also noticed that the components of the task itself were bordering on insignificant in relation to the outcome of the experience.

A family generates a lot of dirty dishes when they are all confined to a small cottage. There is limited hot water and the kitchen space is cramped.

I immediately created a clear order for washing up, with items placed in their set positions. I kept the surfaces around me clear, and performed each action at a calm pace in exactly the same way each day. The repetition was thus a key component.

I discovered the importance of never getting hung up on the amount of dirty dishes that were before me – when I did that, the reluctance felt greater straight away. Negative feelings could be felt and it became even more important to reach the end rather than just doing the dishes. Regardless of the altitude of the towering mountain of dishes, the structure and the method were to remain the same. Presence is found solely in the constituent parts: At first, each piece of porcelain is stained and dirty, but through gentle movement and a little water, the dirt is dissolved and the porcelain is clean and shiny once again. The porcelain is then positioned to dry and you wash up the next items.

In the moments when you are upset and angry, or feel agitated as the result of a feeling and it is difficult to separate your thoughts, a daily exercise like this can dispel your mind's tendency to dwell on such things. You fold your laundry, sort through your possessions, create order for the coming week or do your dishes. The task becomes so clear and straightforward to deal with in such a peaceful state. Presence in a simple everyday act becomes a path to peace with yourself and a way back to a calm and tranquil existence.

Once everything was clean, I felt good. I had been fully there in the moment. I was in control of the situation, and the sub-moments that involved doing the dishes all provided support and protection from disturbed thought patterns and emotional wandering. As if the control of a rushing life was returned to myself. Another important experience was the end point – the actual conclusion was almost completely absent, and the presence spilled over into those activities that I undertook after doing the dishes.

Everything turned into conscious presence instead. Without a beginning. Without an end. In other words, I was able to pick by myself whether I wanted to like doing the dishes or not.

The idea that we have our own choice that lies within each person's heart is a fundamental tenet of Buddhist thought that I am very attached to. The choice is between choosing the positive or the less positive, the good or the less good, love or the absence of love. Doing the dishes is a trivial matter and I don't want to somehow suggest that it is always easy to make those choices in every aspect of life. At some moments in our lives, feelings of hopelessness can be the only healthy reaction. But if you listen carefully enough and you are willing to remain present in what is experienced as resistance or an obstacle to your inner plans, a new interface emerges between the experience of those feelings and your possible reaction, and the remaining emotional state.

Because we all encounter some form of pain in our daily lives, something almost trivial can trigger a powerful emotional storm within us, and in that moment we are not fully in control of our reaction. That's natural. But in the next step we possess the opportunity to make a choice. We can become aware and be ready to take responsibility if we invite compassion and acceptance as our companions on the path to change. If we do that, then even something as simple as doing the dishes can be an act of healing.

53

Breathing Space

'I CAN'T BREATHE,' a yoga student said when she came to a course I was giving on yoga and meditation. Clinically speaking, it was far from an emergency situation, and it goes without saying that she could breathe. On the other hand, the feeling that her breathing was shallow and out of reach, and that it was only with difficulty that it could be deepened and contribute to a pleasing feeling in her body, was quite real. It had also been like that for a long time and had grown into a problem. Breathing happens automatically regardless of our presence or absence. Only for brief moments in our daily lives do we have the thought: I am breathing. But when we completely lose control of how we breathe, and rapid inhalation and exhalation become the norm, the risk of stress increases and we can be filled with an uncomfortable feeling of being crowded.

There is a good reason why books like this one testify to the importance of breathing in an almost nagging way, emphasising it as an inherent resource and stress serum. Regulated breathing has a positive impact on our brain, and deep breaths signal to the body via the vagus nerve that it should be calm and relax. The practical implementation of such breathing methods has long been part of the yoga tradition, and knowledge of some of these techniques can provide effective support in daily life for dealing with stressful situations more effectively.

There is an instruction that leads to the experience that is so simple that you can take it in from this text. While you continue to slowly read on, try to extend your breaths slightly in each breathing cycle. Regardless of whether you are breathing through your nose or mouth, you can experience the effect of breathing in your body. When you reach the end of this paragraph, repeat the following sub-moments: *Breathe in a third of your lung capacity and pause for a moment. Breathe in by another third. Then breathe in fully and hold your breath for a moment once your lungs are completely expanded.*

Then breathe out and repeat these three steps until your lungs are completely empty. Try to keep your body relaxed, and repeat the exercise in full three or four times.

In a passive state and in meditation, I usually take six or seven breaths a minute, while in a stressed situation I take 15 to 25 breaths. In a calm interval, I experience breathing as a deep waveform rather than a quick in-and-out movement. Each part of the breath markedly affects both my body and my mind. Moving to that state gives me the opportunity to experience stillness at more or less any time. A situation like that can be a technique in itself: *Reflex meditation.* If I experience sudden feelings of stress and anxiety within me, then I direct my focus by reflex towards my deep breathing. Just as an athlete uses a trigger to reach a certain state at a given time when it really matters, a stress trigger can be a daily impetus to direct your focus at what calms you. This technique got me accustomed to turning the negative into something positive. When I began experimenting with directly triggered reflex meditation, I noticed after some months that it would happen without me noticing. Stillness came as a reflex.

In a live interview from 2017, Hillary Clinton enthusiastically describes how 'alternate nostril breathing' helped her to keep calm and provided comfort during the intensive period that culminated in her loss in the 2016 US presidential election. 'If you're sitting cross-legged, on the yoga mat, and you're doing it and you're really trying to inhale, and hold it, and then have a long exhale, it is very relaxing.'

The exercise described by Hillary Clinton is a specific exercise known in Sanskrit as *Nadi Shodana.* The exercise involves letting the fingers of one hand close one nostril at a time while the air alternates between the nasal passages. Some of the known effects of the exercise are that it lowers the heart rate and the blood pressure. It is useful that such simple techniques have become available in the mainstream. While sceptics frown and argue that it is a meaningless activity and purely symptomatic of our time, a world of practitioners testify to the valuable, invisible contentment that makes them feel both calm and confident. The breath is the doorway to stillness of both body and breathing. For someone who feels he or she is no longer in harmony with their breath, the opportunity to regain it is opened up. This can be a first step towards steadfast stillness.

Nadi Shodana

Sit or lie in a comfortable position. Bend your index finger and middle finger towards the base of your right thumb. Place your right thumb on your right nostril and block the nasal passage. Breathe in deeply

– draw in a full breath through the left nostril and then immediately block the left nostril using your ring finger and little finger. Release the pressure from your thumb and breathe out through your right nostril. Then breathe in through your right nostril, immediately block the right-hand nasal passage with your thumb and release the pressure on the left-hand side. Repeat at least five times on each side.

59

Feeling Comfort in Change

WHEN I STOP during my everyday life, in a moment that pulls me into safety from the ravages of myself, it is sometimes as if I move to the back row in the cinema and see my own thoughts and emotions projected onto the screen.

Sometimes the film is exciting, sometimes it's pretty boring. Often it is about something that makes me happy and I want it to carry on forever. Not uncommonly, something suddenly happens – a pang of anxiety, a feeling of discomfort – and I wish someone would switch it off. So the film plays on over an infinite number of episodes and one insight is to trust that they will change over time.

Meditation involves making your inner self stable. Stable, in the sense of understanding that your mind is naturally active. You can remain stable and avoid getting stuck watching the film sequences. Without your world ending, you can experience stable clarity both in what is positive and what is negative. You can experience the mechanism of how a feeling takes shape and how it disappears.

As the Trappist monk Thomas Merton put it, 'one of the strange laws of the contemplative life is that in it you do not sit down and solve problems: You bear with them until they somehow solve themselves.'

Because one side of a feeling is precisely that it can take a firm grip on us all, hold on to us and steer us in different directions. Regardless of whether we want that or not. The other side to a feeling is that it changes. Changes constantly. We can test this together. Note a thought or a feeling that appears in your consciousness. Try to follow it for a longer period of time without losing contact. Holding onto a thought opens up new interfaces and gaps between our feelings that give us a different approach to our actions.

Just the other day I received an email. The working day had long since finished, and I remember that for a moment I considered whether to leave reading it until the next day. But I chose to read the message. It was brief, but there was something about the tone – the choice of words and the curt, slightly cool style of the text – that triggered a chain of emotions in me. It was work-related and referred to a meeting that had taken place earlier in the day. The words summoned feelings of agitation and defensiveness within me. In fact, glowing rage briefly took over my mind.

Suddenly, I was no longer in control but was slowly drawn out into speculation and fantasies. I was driven along by emotions that prompted me to act quickly, forcefully and directly. Sharp wording and honed rewrites of what I felt took shape in my head.

Then I suddenly happened to think about a technique that Abraham Lincoln used to use. When he ended up in a similar situation, he would write something he described as a *hot letter*. None of the emotions he felt could be blocked – he would write down whatever he was experiencing within himself at that moment without amendment. But he never sent the letter. Instead, he would put it to one side and wait. He accepted the feeling of anger, but let it take a different direction before finally sensing its decline. The next day, the President would rewrite the letter and send the more thought-through version. In that instance, the words came from somewhere else within him. An impressive exercise in introspection, but also a situation in which the first letter could have had devastating consequences, to say the least.

Once again: One side of a feeling is that it can take hold of us fully, while its other side is that it is subject to change. It appears from nowhere, like a wave rising from the ocean only to return to where it came from after it has broken on the beach. Never again will it be possible to discern it as an isolated part.

When you sit still and do nothing, you can experience a number of waves breaking onto your beach. Just as many have then returned to beneath the ocean surface. The pauses between those waves of emotion become increasingly evident, and experiencing stillness manifests as feeling a core deep within you. Instead of turning away, you turn towards it, and you know that after these feelings there will be other, new feelings which will also change.

Perhaps you think you need to stop being emotional. This is not the case. It's part of your personality. Of course you can keep enjoying things, mourning, laughing, getting goosebumps from great music, benefitting from the rush of love. But the difference is that we don't need to be led away by each and every one of them. We have a choice. This insight can make your everyday life so much easier. Once your mind has become more stable in this way, even unwelcome feelings can become a springboard to lasting security, trust and joy.

65

Changes in Daily Life

HIGH UP ON a shelf in the kitchen of my grandparents' home there was a large white seashell. When I put my ear to its opening, I could hear a loud noise, as if the sea had come ashore and etched itself into the walls of the shell. Every time I visited them in southern Skåne, I would stand on tip-toe to reach the shell on the shelf. Ready to listen. It was always a surprising experience. The rushing sound inside created an image of a horizonless and stormy sea with waves so intense that the dynamics of them merged into a consistently full-bodied roar. An almost deafening constancy of sound welled into my ear canals and made my hearing bones vibrate. Despite the fact that I eventually had the phenomenon explained to me – *well, this is how it works* – I was spellbound; I remained lost in wonder on many occasions at the experience of everything being still and silent. The silence was also to be found in the loudness, and for someone restless perhaps it was easier to hear it right there.

A child needs no next step; rather, everything happens when it happens and what is available comes to life and never requires meaning. But then play becomes a more serious game, and the child's capacity to be here and now is quickly lost. In a time when we are constantly connected, we are instead tugged ever more intensely away from the now. It feels very much more like we're actually on the way to being completely disconnected.

This became clear to me a year or so ago, when I decided to make some minor changes that had an undreamt-of and major impact. Just like everyone else, I'm often connected, which is both rewarding and entertaining in various ways. But increased knowledge of how digital operators exploit various triggers in the brain's reward system in order to actively get us to act in a certain way means I have become more cautious. The digital world offers a chimera of free choice, but in fact our brains are being kidnapped and we don't even know it is happening. The combination of an intelligent interface and smart behavioural scientists transforms our actions in some of the biggest digital arenas into something that is largely predetermined. The seemingly free choice becomes a limitation. But it's not just that: We are not always satisfied with the choices that we make for ourselves.

According to American studies, we use our mobiles for 4.7 hours per day, of which several hours are spent on the major social media platforms. Another study conducted by the Centre for Humane Technology that looked at 200,000 participants identified that more than half stated they were dissatisfied with how they spent this freely chosen time on digital platforms. Your own choice has created a type of behaviour that is hard to break and, what is even worse, leads to self-reproach. We continue to consume even though we are no longer hungry. Doped by smart design. Increasingly disconnected. Increasingly absent.

I decided to create interfaces and time zones in my home. A *media fast* in order to rest my brain muscles.

The first thing that happened was that I became more attentive to the transition between doing and being. The transition between the outer environment and the inner. When I came home, I wanted to create a clear boundary and stop for a while, to enable me to put things that might distract me to one side. I began to engage in a *do-nothing-activity*, like sitting down for a bit in a comfy armchair and just reflecting on things. Quite simply, a place to set down the day that had passed. Perhaps a final thought about something that was lingering on and needed to be brought to a conclusion. But also in order to be present with my family.

There is an incredible difference between this and coming home while leaving half of yourself in the outer world. If you have kids, they will notice the difference in the way you listen.

Even more importantly, I began to switch off my phone and computer earlier in the evenings, turn them on later in the mornings, and I never took any form of electronics into the bedroom. In order to enable the last of these initiatives, I bought an analogue alarm clock. Yes – they still exist, and they work perfectly.

The impact was immediate and verging on amazing. When I left my digital devices, vast swathes of time were freed up – more than it was possible to efficiently measure. I didn't realise how much free time screen time had robbed me of, but also how much mental time it had taken up afterwards that was focused on what I had experienced during the time at my screen.

When someone called after me, I no longer had to ask them to wait or even feel a degree of irritation. In the early days, those impulses were still noticeably there. A hand reaching for a phone without any idea at all what I was going to do with it.

When I went to bed in the evening, the desire to read books returned to me. Reading a book can be an occupation, but it is completely different from endlessly scrolling through the Internet. A book has a final chapter; a book only has a finite number of pages. The Internet never ends. The wonderful feeling of finishing something now gave me a blessed, stress-free end to the day. Screen time was replaced with intervals in which creativity once again had room to blossom. When I no longer had anything to do during longer, continuous periods of time, more and more ideas began to come to me. Like on all those days when I was little and there was nothing to do. Just like many mothers of that era, my mum had an unassailable confidence in the benefits of being outside as soon as the clouds dispersed. I remember many occasions where I wandered up and down the street we lived on, sat down or hung around on the pavement and hoped a friend would turn up. Being bored was one of the best things I could experience. Being bored is a springboard to creativity. This was the conclusion of researchers in a British study in any case. They asked participants to perform a series of transparently dull tasks, such as reading old-fashioned paper-based telephone books. Once they had completed these tasks, they were encouraged to think of as many ideas as possible for an ordinary plastic cup. According to the study, those people who had performed the boring task came up with significantly more creative ideas than the control group.

Another team of researchers found evidence that people who were bored more easily developed altruistic traits. In their bored state, they expressed a feeling of meaninglessness. It transpires that this can help us to try and recreate meaning through doing things like donating blood or giving money to charity.

Resting Your Hands

OUR HANDS ARE often busy in our daily lives. Phones and computers still remain largely dependent on our hand movements to operate them, or as support when we are lying down and looking at them. Sometimes, restless hands can be a sign that you are experiencing stress or discomfort, and I have noted on many occasions how people who are meditating scratch themselves more frequently at the beginning of their meditation session. Our hands need to rest.

As a standalone meditative exercise, you can rest them on your knees, let them be completely passive and just experience their light weight and the points of contact between your hands and legs. Resting your hands becomes an impetus towards stillness and a clear interruption of active doing. When your hands are resting, you can bring together your thumb and forefinger on each hand. This movement should be so light that you only just notice the point of contact. Maintain this presence and let the skin contact remain the same for a while. Don't press harder and don't let your fingers lose contact.

Can you let your hands rest for a while every day?

73

Being at One with Listening

ONCE WE HAVE begun to find our ability to stop a little, the opportunity to let the still breathing space gradually spill over into all activities in our daily lives is presented to us.

One such opportunity may be to learn to listen in a new way. For example, listening in deep presence when another person is talking to you. Instead of listening, we often seem to be preparing our next response rather than taking in what is being said in the moment – as if we already know what is going to be said before the sentence reaches its end. Listening deeply requires you to be properly silent.

Many years ago, I studied linguistics at university. We were split into groups of four in order to carry out a conversation exercise. Another male student and I were tasked with discussing with two female students what summer meant to us. The subject was irrelevant, but the half-hour-long conversation was recorded and then transcribed in full. The transcription included all the words uttered, as well as all particles like 'hmm' and 'yes' and 'oh' and 'ah-ha'.

Afterwards, we had to analyse the text, which was a painful process. It became apparent that we listened carelessly to the end of another person's utterance. We discovered that we all added particles and emphasising *yes*es during the time someone else was talking, but that these indicated different meanings. Sometimes, such a word really did mark a genuine confirmation and positive affirmation: *What you are saying is interesting.* But on many occasions it was just an interrupting marker that mostly meant: *Get to the point, I've got something more interesting to say.* Unfortunately, it was we men who were responsible for the majority of the latter.

Another way of listening is absorptive listening, where you make eye contact, show an active interest in what is being said and encourage the person speaking to express their thoughts. Engagement that opens the door to dialogue. From there, listening can be deepened further. It can become an action that alleviates another person's suffering. The person speaking gets to relieve themselves of whatever burdens them.

You don't have to agree with what is being said – but you should still listen with generous solicitude, without interrupting or correcting. When you feel the need to do so – perhaps with good advice – opt to remain in silent presence instead. Rest your tongue and absorb what is being said like a sponge. This can have a positive healing effect on the speaker, and sometimes it is worth more than good advice and wisdom.

Try it the next time you are talking to your child or a friend. Switch off your phone and adopt the still position of the listener. Remember that the speaker should be allowed to reach their point in their own time. Leave a pause before you reply, if a reply is even necessary. Hear the speaker's words without emerging from your silence. Hear them ring out. Back to the silence.

As it is said in a Buddhist recitation:

> 'We shall practise listening so attentively that we are able to hear what the other is saying – and also what is left unsaid. We know that by listening deeply we already alleviate a great deal of pain and suffering in the other.'

77

Pauses

Let's bring this chapter to a close with a final exercise. All I ask you to do is to pay more attention to the pauses between my words.

Listen to the silence. Experience the silence between the words as longer and longer pauses occur.

In these intervals is where

the silence

and

the stillness

are to be

found.

II.

Nature

81

A Tree in My Garden

BRANCHES, A THIN layer of snow in the clefts, emerging winter buds, even an abandoned bird's nest. Although I live a long way from the wilderness, I can still contemplate the ageing maple in our courtyard with the same wonder you can experience deep in the forest. A glimpse of something bigger, simplified, and simultaneously the expression of fragility. If it were to be taken away, there would be nothing natural left to see from my window. Merely structures and environments created by humans. Looking at the tree is not only an experience of beauty, it also offers a sense of unity between two transient lives. A movement among the sprawling branches, a sluggish blackbird heaves itself out and disappears from my field of vision, and like a reservoir of silence the trunk remains still while the thinnest twigs sway.

Zen Buddhist literature describes how smaller buildings were erected in proximity to or amidst nature. A so-called Zen do – or viewing room – just a few square metres in size. If you were to see such a building from a distance, it would be barely visible to the naked eye – it would be well-camouflaged beneath a tree or merged into the landscape by other means. The interior of such a building is minimalist, with only a few furnishings and accessories. Instead, it is considered part of nature itself: The person who is within it can see herbs and greenery growing out of the soil, and due to the proximity they also feel their own life being lived.

The sense of unity with the external is reinforced through the low floor, positioned at the same level as the ground outside. A structure that obscures the distinguishing features of nature and human to the greatest possible extent. 'There is indeed a strange and profound satisfaction in feeling this consciousness of identity between your own transitory life and the transitory life of other earth-products, whether organic or inorganic,' as the author John Cowper Powys described the co-dependent relationship between humans and nature.

For me, being close to what is growing is in all its forms soothing and an antidote to exhaustion and overload. It seems to be a generally held view, as well as something that has received scientific support.

Several research reports point to the healing effect of nature. Perhaps it is in my capacity as a resident of an area dominated by asphalt that my imagination is so keenly caught by these studies. At the University of Exeter Medical School, they noted after large-scale analysis that there were clear correlations between the proximity of urban dwellers to green spaces and long-term improvements in mental health. Improvements in health that (it transpired) lasted for up to three years.

Other studies show us that the brain reacts by reducing stress levels when we are in nature. Even passively being in areas with trees and grass makes us calmer, and has a beneficial and strengthening impact on us.

Even those who can't go out into the natural landscape can be positively influenced. A team of researchers studied how inmates at a prison in Oregon reacted to video exposure to nature. Two groups of 24 participated. One group was given the opportunity to work out up to five times per week, while the other got to work out but also got to go to a dedicated room to watch a 45-minute-long nature film.

Mood, stress levels and the number of incidents of violence were all tracked for one year. The results were remarkable. Inmates who had consumed the depictions of nature felt calmer – but most significantly, they were involved in 26 per cent fewer violent incidents during the study.

When your senses – amidst the noise and pollution – get hold of the silence of nature and its nuances, you once again become whole. It requires so little – all you have to do is sometimes turn your attention to the silence.

And when you stay in it, the silence requires nothing in return. Instead of running all over the place, I often go nowhere, so that I can hear the silence in the maple outside my window. The ageing trunk reaches up, its branches silhouetted against the sky. Day has turned to early evening, and in the darkness a pair of doves roost on one of the larger branches. The silence seems to flood through their motionless bodies.

Further away, I can hear the city.

But much closer to me, nature is present.

In the shape of one single tree.

87

A Movement Towards Stillness

I TAKE THE green line on the Stockholm metro, heading west. The trip from my home in Stockholm city centre to my destination only takes around 20 minutes. The train winds slowly out of the city, but nothing during my journey reminds me of where I'm going: The buildings don't thin out, the volume of traffic doesn't sink – in fact it gets heavier when we emerge into daylight, leaving the tunnels behind. The movement relative to what is still remains constant.

After a brief walk from the metro station I find myself on a footpath in a nature reserve. Quick, uncomplicated steps forward soon turn into a growing sense for my footing. There are roots, small protruding stones and the odd insect pottering across the path. I find my stride and begin to walk properly – a natural movement in which I know when to move my foot forward and how to place it on the ground.

My upper body is affected by the elasticity of my feet against the ground and feels more relaxed, and my senses become open to scents and sounds. Only now have I completely left the city behind and truly arrived in the woods.

Trees enclose me on each side, arch after arch opening in towards the deeper part of the forest. Arches created by greenery – when you look into one of them it is peculiar how the light is kept out, and a soft darkness pervades. Today there is barely another person on this footpath through nature, and I continue onwards for a while, feeling a breeze fanning my face – the air streaming in and out of my nostrils.

The steady rhythm of my steps and the density of my breathing means that no other thoughts can get in. It becomes so very clear how and when my perspective shifts and becomes a direct reflection of the calm of nature. It is as if I leave my heavy, daily baggage at the outer limits of the path while continuing on in the company of the gentle breeze.

If someone were to give an example of a place that provides silence, the forest would be an obvious one. But the reality is almost the opposite: If you crouch down to the level of the grass on a summer's day, the whirr of flying insects can be deafening, with a noctuid bouncing against a cow parsnip the size of my hand and the rustle of the birch leaves. A pause under the forest tree-cover can allow you to discover a dynamic auditory experience that only offers absolute silence for brief moments.

But it is another pleasant soothing wall of sound, and if you want to quickly find calm in your body, then it is well worth familiarising yourself with the art of sound meditation. It is simple, specific and rapidly provides a bedrock of presence to relax against. To start with, lifting my feet high and walking with determined steps, I go a little further into the increasingly darker parts of the forest. In one of the arches, the sparse light that passes through the tree canopy is easier to make out – it shines ethereally down onto tufts of grass, as if there might be some valuable object on the ground. It is impossible to fully grasp – there is no visible order and there is no point in trying to inventorise the wooded space in which I find myself. This disorder, naturally covered in undergrowth, has always made me calm.

I sharpen my attention with a couple of long breaths, which then automatically remain slow and unremarkable. I then choose to note one of the sounds of the forest in further detail: Is its volume strong or faint, dynamic or constant, indistinct or sharp, powerful or small and thin? How does it vary during the time that I listen to it? How do the sounds travel? Where do they come from? Where are they going?

I then shift my attention to another sound and repeat the exercise. Layers of sounds are uncovered and enter my zone of attention one by one. Soon, I am able to interchange between listening to several sounds at once or one at a time, experiencing how I can decide where to direct my focus. There is a freedom in this for the overloaded mind. Here, the random, impulsive wandering thoughts cease; my experience of the sounds around me is free from the chains of association and provides me with an unbelievably detailed experience of the forest.

One single thing at a time: A woodpecker drumming, a crescendo of wind through the trembling foliage of the aspen, a diffuse sound far away that stops completely after a while, the sound of my breathing close by. A blackbird whispers *Be kind to yourself and others.* I let the seeds of compassion germinate within me, and I think about how the old Buddhist texts sometimes refer to loosening the grip on oneself and remaining in a state of perception. In its deepest form, it can be perceived as a pleasant gap – a rare emptiness, as if something stops still when everything around it changes. I'm still unable to get much closer to the experience. But if I understand correctly, something is always left behind afterwards – a perpetual residue, a foundation that always seems to stand still when everything is hurrying and in change. It is worth all the effort of meditation, and the door is never fully closed. If you have lowered your bucket all the way down once, you are familiar with the depth and not afraid of it either. When you once again re-encounter the noise and emotional storms of daily life that can sometimes be mistaken for being all of you, you know that the other exists – keeping you steady.

The airy sounds of the meadows, the sounds of the forest, the sounds of breathing and the sounds that have no name – none of these demand an advanced technique for stopping in the unconditional, unforced moment: An important moment, where a stroke of insight can flow in through the act of meditation. Instead of being too attached to pleasure, you understand the relationship with the past and embrace its bittersweet beauty.

The path back is just as long, but now your vision is clear, the substance of your breaths moving gently at the bottom of each exhalation. The almost-blooming lupins tempt you with their bright pink colour as the wind bends them sideways. A bird of prey soars over the tree tops, gliding along on the air currents. And then it disappears.

93

The Fixed Point

KVARKEN AND SURROUNDING *areas west three to eight, Landsort northwest two, Gulf of Finland southerly wind eight to 12, tonight changing to northwest around five. German Bight south seven, Southern Sea of Bothnia three to seven. From tonight south rising and good visibility.*

The shipping forecast is emitted monotonously from the radio. My mother, father, sister and I are listening so attentively that we are staring into space and any unwanted sound receives a *hush!* in response. This is long before the 'doing lots of things at once era' and we are sitting completely still in the cabin of the boat. We are a long way out in the Stockholm archipelago, and will soon find out whether it will be possible to sail on in the morning or whether we will end up stuck in harbour for another couple of days.

Southern Utsire easterly wind seven, tomorrow increasing one to four with good visibility. The monotony of the voice makes me slip into daydreams. In my imagination, I am sailing to those beautiful names: The

Archipelago Sea, German Bight and on northeast towards the cliffs of the Weather Islands. All these places feel like home territory. I am obviously maintaining a firm grip on the tiller, so as not to fall down into the cockpit as the waves strike. On my boat the *Gypsy Moth*, soaked to my skin, the taste of salt in my mouth. I stretch up in a practised movement to check the horizon, reefing the sail as a new wave attacks the boat's bow.

The voice on the radio mentions Hanö and Utklippan and the wind figure is below the magical limit. Mum's and Dad's eyes meet. We have been given the information we need – a sigh of relief – yet we still remain there, listening to the mesmeric voice. We sway in time with the rhythm of the mantra: *Harstena southwest five, poor visibility, Gotska Sandön southerly wind seven to nine, falling, Svenska Högarna and Söderarm two, Kemi lighthouse northwest five.*

Four times daily for a period of 40 years, Peter Jefferson read the shipping forecast on BBC Radio. It is said that his departure from the role in 2009 was connected to his barely audible utterance of a profanity beginning with 'f' while on air. However, it seems more likely that the reason was Jefferson's recent cancer diagnosis, and that the decision to leave the role was his own. Listeners immediately missed his radio presence and the reaction didn't take long to emerge. Many listeners described how his shipping forecast had lulled them to sleep at night. Almost none of the listeners had visited the places recited, but they had somehow become part of their lives. The feeling of belonging became a buoy to which all listeners could moor themselves when the wind picked up. A few years ago, Jefferson made a new recording of the shipping forecast after his lengthy absence. This time it was in an altogether different context – and during the introduction he promises 'unusually calm weather conditions'. An American company behind one of the biggest meditation apps on the globe had invited Jefferson to record a shipping forecast in his familiar monotone to support a relaxation exercise. He cautiously encourages the listener to take a couple of deep breaths, ease off and simply listen to the weather conditions in these remote places. His shipping forecast has become a true bedtime story for adults.

In 2018 in Sweden, radio listeners were polled on whether the shipping report should continue to be broadcast on Sveriges Radio, the equivalent of the BBC. It is broadcast five times each day, using up several minutes of radio airtime. A large proportion of listeners wanted to keep the daily feature and some said it was a 'stress ball' that had almost become a form of meditation for them. Another said that it was relaxing to listen 'to a presenter... reading out things I don't need to have an opinion on.'

I told a friend about the survey. Her face lit up and said: 'It's like listening to poetry.'

Well, perhaps there is something about the rhythm that gives you a feeling of stillness. Perhaps we feel an affiliation with something greater than ourselves. From a distance, we can feel kinship with the 209 inhabitants of Utsira and with the lighthouse keeper sitting alone in his cabin on the Utklippan islands listening to find out whether the harsh wind is going to drop. It could have been us, and we feel it with him.

Listening at a distance, we are provided with an illusory fixed point to hold on to. When the world around us feels insecure and miserable, there is something that is still the same.

We all find our own ways to the restful stillness. Even when there is a northerly wind blowing at 20 knots and rising in Fisher.

99

The Ghost Park

TODAY, MY HEAD has been far too full of thoughts, which have somehow been turned into a dull lowness. I'm on my way home from work and decide to rest for a while. I'm not actually in that much of a hurry. It occurs to me what a slight shift changing my plans is and what a big impetus in the opposite direction the change can have as it takes shape in that moment. From the thought 'I don't really have time for this' to an approach and a decision takes very little effort in comparison to the effect obtained.

The very name of this park appeals to me: Spökparken or 'the Ghost Park'. Described as a baroque garden, it is certainly not a park that you happen upon in passing. Proud maples are comfortably spaced out, some of the trunks leaning over the path – and the treetops form a roof over my head above the bench I choose to sit down on. A shadow forms a clear line on the paving stones. One of Stockholm's busiest streets is rumbling just a stone's throw away, the city refusing to be silent but never able to drown out the inner silence. It's late afternoon on a normal weekday and the large number of visitors to the park surprises me. Several are looking down at their phones, but I notice that about half – just like me – aren't doing anything at all. Just sitting there and looking at the park.

Often when we stop, our brains continue at full pelt. Thoughts rush by and sometimes you can clearly experience them as more unruly as we begin to become more aware. Everyone who meditates will be familiar with this, so don't feel downhearted. Instead, consider your intense flow of thoughts and your feelings with kindness and wonder: 'As an old man or woman who watches as a child plays.' If you regularly practise, the rushing waterfall of your thoughts will soon turn into an eager brook and eventually into a rushing river heading out to sea. Waves that become ripples will eventually stop moving on a warm, still ocean surface.

I decide to do an exercise here on the park bench. We can call it 'letting go', and it is an effective technique for quickly opening the window to your inner self and clearing your mind of the day's tasks.

It is neither particularly difficult nor demanding, but one requirement is that you do not block or ignore your thoughts – instead, you should observe and note your thoughts, which are to continue moving freely. Simply pay attention to each thought without hindering it, experience how it affects you and then release it. In order to make things easier, you can use a kind of label – a symbolic word. Let's use the word *pass*. The word becomes a reminder not to get entangled in the thought, and it also helps the thought to fade away and disappear. You let the word become a protective mantle. If it suits you better, you can repeat the word more regularly. But ensure it is always softly, and not in any way repelling. Throughout the exercise, your eyes can remain open and your body should be positioned comfortably.

A child's counting before they head off to look for their friends in a game of hide and seek is a good signal to stop my exercise. I look at the time and barely 20 minutes have passed since I came into the park. The line of the shadow on the paving is gone and an ethereal layer of cloud conceals the patch of sky visible between the trees. I cycle slowly homewards, thinking about a few lines that the mystic Hjalmar Ekström once wrote: 'Without peace, the heart is like a bird with its wings clipped – feebly flapping without getting off the spot. With peace, its power and mobility are unlimited.'

103

Towards Silence

SOMETIMES WE FILL ourselves with too much. We are so full we can no longer hear the silence. Do we want to shut out or stifle our feelings?

Over the course of a few days, I have the opportunity to be alone in close proximity to nature. Early in the morning, I step out into the bitingly cold landscape. It takes just a few minutes of strolling before I find myself surrounded by complete silence.

I walk along a snow-covered forest path, and when I intuitively stop it occurs to me that my movements are the only sound that exist in the landscape in which I find myself. The density of the silence is so intense it is like a loud shout. I burst out into an unconscious *wow*. At first, I laugh and perhaps the laugh slips out as an indicator of position in the flowing silence. Or perhaps it was just the cry of joy of a city dweller starved of silence? A moment in which there is nothing to add and nothing needs to be removed, and I remain standing in silence. Speechless. The trees and I, both still.

In my immobility, I assimilate fully with the silence, barely able to break it by continuing my movement forward. Comfortably paralysed in it. Like a deep friendship. The forest is silent. The path is silent. There is nothing in the distance. Everything feels familiar and as it should be.

When I was 20 years old, I travelled to South Asia for the first time. I went to India to visit Karma, my parents' sponsor child and my 'brother', a few years my senior. At the time, he lived in northwestern India in an area with the lovely name of Happy Valley. A few years earlier, he had visited us in Sweden, and now I was travelling to the country where he and a large number of other Tibetans in exile had grown up. I got to see India before the Internet and mobile phones, when handwritten letters were the channel of communication with Sweden.

After a month or so in the country, we decided to visit the Valley of Flowers. This spectacular valley, 13,000 feet above sea level, is beautifully situated and surrounded by snow-covered glaciers. The proximity to Tibet appealed to us – we were separated by just a single mountain. But, as the name suggests, the valley is better known for its hundreds of different varieties of flowers. Inaccessible and hidden to the world up until the 1930s, it is also still home to the shy snow leopard. As a cliché, I was reading Peter Matthiessen's *The Snow Leopard* at the time, which reinforced the mystique around the rocky mountains: 'The search may begin with a restless feeling, as if one were being watched. One turns in all directions and sees nothing. Yet one senses that there is a source for this deep restlessness; and the path that leads there is not a path to a strange place, but the path home.'

After almost a month in India, I was in pretty bad shape. In a short space of time I had lost more than 7 kilos and I should have stayed in the plains. But high on India's colourful chaos, I couldn't get enough and we had advanced at a rapid pace. We set off from the mountain village of Ghangaria at dawn in order to reach the Valley of Flowers and make it back before sunset. A beautiful path alongside a rushing mountain river led us slowly towards the valley. It was August and the heat was oppressive, despite the monsoon. The hike was not particularly challenging, but we stopped with increasing frequency – dipping our towels into the ice-cold water before putting them on our heads to cool off. When we raised our gazes, we could make out in the distance the protruding cliffs, the orange-clad hermits sitting still in the position of meditation.

In the days prior to this, we had looked for bliss in the glittering waters of the Ganges, haggled as tourists with the traders in Rishikesh, and almost like in Roald Dahl's *The Wonderful Story of Henry Sugar* been offered divine magic for an affordable price. Now, with a sky that felt increasingly closer to our heads, the hustle and bustle of the city seemed distant. Exhausted, we finally reached the Valley of Flowers and I remember Karma's first remark: 'On the other side is Tibet.' He had probably never been that close to his home country in his adult years. We dropped onto the grass covered in flowers. I had never experienced anywhere like it and the lingering silence was nothing but liberating. I was as far from home as I had ever been, but in the middle of the silence I felt at home. The familiar tranquillity. The same silence that had carried me through the woods around my home city on so many occasions.

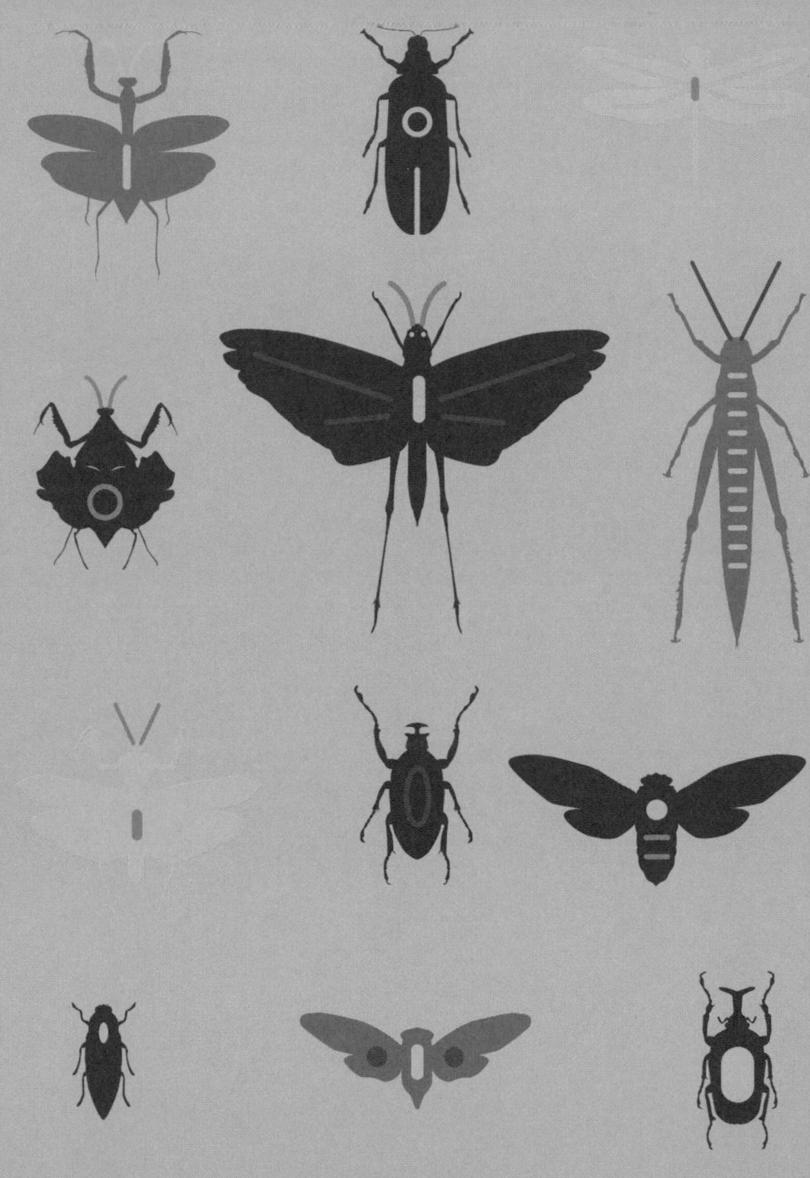

109

In Silence

THERE IS A poem by the late American poet William Stafford in which he writes:

> 'My father could hear a little animal step,
> or a moth in the dark against the screen,
> and every far sound called the listening out
> into places where the rest of us had never been.'

The poet goes on to wish that he could invite in the quiet, '...waiting for a time when something in the night will touch us too from that other place.'

Not only is there a pleasant tranquillity in those words, but there is also something that says that silence is an act, rather than just the quality of an environment. It is a humble attitude and something that we don't have to wait for; rather it is a place to which we can invite ourselves and others.

Being able to remain in silence and self-reflection is a joy in our often hectic daily lives.

For me, the early mornings are my daily quiet place. No one in our home has woken up – not even our cat – and the only sounds audible from outside are pleasing ones: A distant bird's repetitive call, a door opening and closing somewhere far away. To me, these early mornings mean yoga and meditation. I usually begin by sitting on a chair with my legs crossed, looking out of the window for a while, noting the weather, the nuances in the sky and perhaps a special way in which light or shade falls on the façade of the building opposite ours. That early morning has a calming effect on my body. Sleep has barely left me and few thoughts have begun to take its place.

When you incorporate the calm of morning into your body, peaceful meditation almost comes by itself. On those days where it doesn't, I move systematically from:

The body's sensations – I observe whether there is any tension anywhere and whether I can relieve this by being aware of the muscles in the relevant area. Then I make my breathing quiet and calm. Sometimes it can help to perceive your breathing as a circular movement, where the transition between exhalation and inhalation is soft – almost erased entirely. All because the body is silent.

Speech – I find relaxation in the roof of my mouth, letting words leave my body and inviting in silence. An immense sense of liberation forms. A freedom from seeking things to say, allowing me instead to let everything rest in enveloping silence.

The mind – when my body has fallen silent, I finally let my mind rest in a spacious, natural state of equilibrium in which I keep myself relaxed no matter what I hear, what I see, what I feel. Nothing is measured or judged by descriptors such as 'good' or 'bad'. My body is relaxed, my mind is relaxed, no matter what it feels.

This moment sets the tone for my day – a feeling that each morning is once again put together and reborn. I always finish each meditation in an atmosphere of benevolence and tolerance. If I still cling to negative patterns such as irritation or jealousy, I try to say that I wish others well and describe what is good.

115

The Greatest Possible Silence

THE PHILOSOPHER MAX PICARD wrote in his 1920 book *The World of Silence* that: 'The radio has occupied the whole space of silence... There is no silence any longer. Even when the radio is turned off the radio-noise still seems to go on inaudibly.' And the world hardly seems to have become a quieter place since then. We are constantly called upon, even chased: Text messages, notifications, advertising. Different temptations away from silence. We are encouraged to speak out, exist by breaking our silence, and our daily lives are literally such a cacophony of sounds that an increasing number of people hear the call of silence.

With large headphones covering our ears, more and more of us are encountering daily life in a noise-reduced world. There are too many sounds and impressions – they are too intense, and increasingly often I find that silence is my refuge. One early morning a week or so ago, the metro was covered in advertising for a supplier of health experiences: *Share in the stillness.* While planning a trip to Finland, I encounter the following heading on the website: *Silence, please*. Messages which are tempting because we know that that is what we are looking for, but which also that tell us that silence has become a luxury. Something that those who can afford it can share. But in conversations, in nature, in music and in meditation, silence is freely present everywhere. It is unmistakable and makes you feel its meaning, even though silence itself has no purpose whatsoever.

Silence is more than the absence of sound. More than the absence of language. It is a fundamental structure that emerges when we leave space for it. By making your body still and listening in the quiet spaces, listening to what is happening instead of to your interpretations of what is happening, you can notice the silence. In some ways, it is just pure existence and impossible to represent other than as a reflection of its effect.

Silence sometimes has to be rediscovered. It is hidden in the intervals of our busy daily lives, intervals that seem to be increasingly cut off. All too often, things merge together and end up adhering to each other. Just as intervals in the flow of social media are non-existent, the intervals between an opinion and an opposing view are now just a rapid bounce. Everything is caught on the volley and speaking is seemingly more exciting than listening.

In the world of poetry, the space of silence is more clearly opened to me. I notice that it often becomes my refuge. It feels liberating and undisturbed and vitalising to stay there. Surfaces are left deliberately blank on the sheet of paper. A blank page that speaks to the reader in a different way. The intense stream of words naturally becomes single syllables before once again elastically expanding. A stripped-down, taut form with free syntax can lead the reader to reflective silence without any counter-demands. This is the case in a poem by Gunnar Björling in his collection *Du går de ord* (You Go the Words):

'That shadows
wordlessness
Till that is
and silence.'

The poet with a pad of paper before them, in the moment before writing the poem, is empty. There is the possibility of filling the sheet with words. Another is to decline, and not to write. The tip of a pen standing still. A hand trembling. The reader is cradled into this.

In Japanese culture, a living space that exists between two entities is known as *ma*. I talk to the artist Ninia Sverdrup, whose reflections on the perception of time took her to Japan to better understand how these two letters influenced a society where the concept seems obvious and things lose their value in the absence of *ma*.

According to Ninia Sverdrup, *ma* occurs in the pure, reflective and necessary space found between two structures. This gap is full of possibilities, such as during a conversation when someone finishes a point – and there is a gap before the other person replies. There is a live interface dependent on the two interlocutors' presence, where things have the opportunity to germinate. In karate, *ma* is the ability to be present in the perfect space between oneself and one's opponent. But perhaps the most beautiful example of *ma* is the perfectly kept distance between two people who are about to kiss each other.

The language of music contains several forms of pauses that create this interval: An interval of silence, when the music rhythm and structure are interrupted. Classical music is filled with examples, such as in the Finnish composer Jean Sibelius's 'Symphony no. 5', where the final six offset chords surround an effective silence. It is an interval that goes beyond rhythm, and instead of being 'hit' by the instrument movements, my alertness is shifted to what is happening between the massive chords. The pauses. Close your eyes and listen!

In the Finnish composer Arvo Pärt's 'Tabula Rasa II Silentium', silence is experienced as present throughout the entire listening experience despite the absence of actual pauses. Silence is both a constant and a basis for the music. It is lingering, as the strings weave a fragile net from just a few varying tones that are more in parallel with silence than with breaking it. The piece, which has become the only thing I have listened to as I wrote this book, provides a feeling of resting in silence throughout the instruments' precise articulation and interactions. The composition was first performed to an audience in 1977. The Estonian composer Erkki-Sven Tüür was in the audience and describes the experience as a feeling that eternity had touched him through the music. I think I can understand what he felt. When the piece ended and everything returned to absolute silence, Tüür says it was as if no one in the audience wanted to interrupt by clapping.

Even clearer is the silence in the introduction to Fugazi's 'Waiting Room'. The song, with a punk guitar riff, is interrupted in the middle of ramping up – and is followed by a completely unexpected silence of almost five seconds, which creates a contrasting tension and reinforcement of the song's title. If you turn up the volume, you can hear that the band are still there – a guitarist touching a string. The listener is invited in and a common energy is gathered and intensified when the song once again resumes. The pauses, the intervals, become a centralised gathering point but also the starting position where something powerful can begin afresh.

That is exactly how I experience the contemplative pause. It is at once a landing and a rebirth, an interface that gathers power, concentrated in its form. From it emanates action, strength and creativity.

So, in silence, an attentive interval stretches out between the last words said and those who make themselves part of the silence. A necessary interval that is carefully observed by those who humbly listen. An emptiness where promises as yet unfulfilled and undreamt-of opportunities can appear.

You can experience silence like that everywhere.

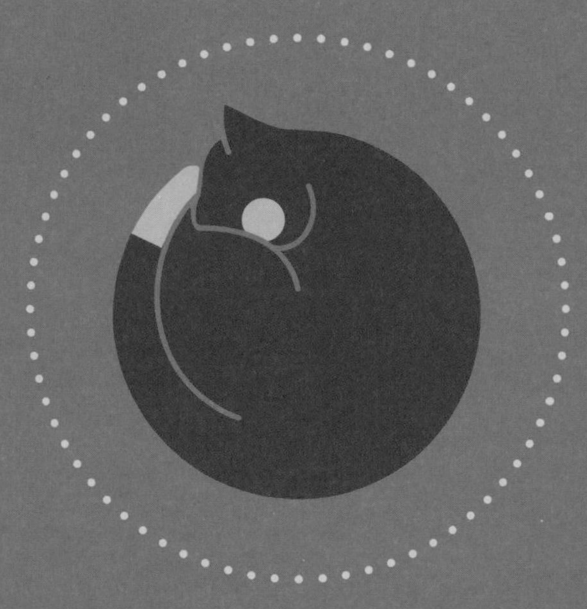

121

Silence Is

WHEN I WAS younger, I thought stillness was easier to find in remote places. In remote countries, preferably shrouded in mystery. Stillness required a physical transfer from one place to another, subject to external circumstances.

When, in spite of everything, I sometimes managed to find it, it was important keep anything that might interrupt the moment out of the way, by keeping the outside world at a distance and blocking what might seem disruptive. Like standing frozen to the spot when you encounter a wild animal in the forest. You know that the moment you move, the animal will bound away. Vanish.

Nowadays, within the perspective of what I experienced during contemplation, I find stillness a constant presence – our innermost room of consciousness. Only once I had travelled the entire world without truly finding stillness did I understand that it had never been further away than my ability to focus my presence on the letters *n* and *o* and *w*. By maintaining my attention and allowing a steady equanimity instead of immediately acting, a shift occurs to an experience of silence and stillness. And when we experience our inner stillness, we maintain contact with ourselves. The ancient text *Bhagavadgita* sets out the recipe even more clearly: 'Be the same in action as in adversity: Such equanimity is called yoga.'

As I write this, our black cat appears out of nowhere. Despite her stiff joints, she still jumps smoothly and confidently up to lie down next to me on the sofa. As the French renaissance writer Montaigne put it, 'When I play with my cat, how do I know that she is not playing with me rather than I with her?'

Nowadays, she often lies close beside me. She has grown old. It is almost a decade since we re-homed her from the cat rescue centre – terrified, distraught and starved of love and security.

I put the palm of my hand on one of her paws. She lifts her other paw and rests it on the back of my hand. After a minute or so, she will settle down after adjusting the upper part of her body, intensely tensing her leg muscles before eventually relaxing completely.

I experience my own deeper breathing in relation to the cat's shallow breaths. I feel my ribcage expanding and compressing in a steady rhythm.

123

The three letters *n* and *o* and *w* are connected together and silence descends around us. Everything settles into a marvellous stillness. A silence comfortably enveloping me for just as long as I choose to remain in the zone of presence and equanimity.

125

Forest Bathing – Shinrin-yoku

THE FOREST IS silent today and we stop talking. An agreed silence. It is part of the forest walk.

Walking meditation comes naturally to me on the forest path. It is a natural way to move and when I place my feet on the ground, that is where my presence is. I leave the walking from point A to point B, and find myself instead in the step. After just a couple of steps in presence, you realise it is a way that leads you away from pondering. Presence is found almost wholly in this step – the weight on the ground and the gentle movement. It's not enough for anything else. Walking meditation moves the practice of meditation one step into ongoing life and for anyone finding seated meditation difficult it can be more accessible. The first steps feel awkward, but soon they are coordinated with the rhythm of breathing. The posture of the body becomes more upright, chest lifted, and I note how many steps I take per inhalation. My shoulders sink, my head is raised and I count how many steps I take on the subsequent exhalation. There is no need to remind yourself to be present – just let the counting of the steps follow the natural pace of your breathing. It soon becomes a flowing rhythm. During each step I feel how my heel hits the grounds, my toes spread and push off from the ground – my legs stretch and my stomach muscles tense. Body and mind become one. Unconsciously, my pace has slowed and I experience an almost soundless walk on a path leading through the yellow and brown leaves scattered on the ground. My counting stops and one inhalation becomes one step – one exhalation the next. My presence feels increasingly obvious, my body increasingly effortless. My thoughts die down and I can clearly experience nature in every step. Finally, a mantra whispers through my body and through my mind: 'Breathe in, my whole body in still presence. Breathe out, my whole body in still presence.'

The path I am following reaches an end and a stile takes me over a stone wall.

On the other side the path widens into a gravel track. I stand still and look around. In a field a little way off there are four horses that look as though they are parallel parked – perfectly still. Even further away, there is a wall of pine that lacks all dimension in the afternoon light. They seem to be put in place, flat against the backdrop of the sky.

All my worries have left me.

As if an eraser has been rubbed carefully over the pencil marks on a sheet of paper, like disappearing footprints in moist leaves on a forest path, all my anxiety has left me.

120

The Tree

I LOOK OUT of the kitchen window. I see the same tree. The bare branches adorned with yellow flowers. The same maple in a different season. A daily pause from the constant stream of impressions, whims and associations.

The enclosed nature of the city or the wilder kind: They both heal us hyperactive people in the here and now. If you can't physically be present, then a meditation method – so-called visualisation – with nature as its object can be particularly suitable for situations where there is stress and tension.

First of all, take a couple of deep breaths to get your body to relax and give you peace of mind. Then place a light presence against the flow of your natural breathing.

Imagine a picture of an open landscape – perhaps somewhere you have been before. A place you like. Look at the ground beneath your feet, see the colours and feel the familiar scents. Take your time.

Imagine that you are directing your gaze up to the sky. What colour is the sky?

Is there no breeze, or are the clouds moving across the sky?

Then summon a picture of a solitary tree growing in the landscape.

Close your eyes for a while and see the tree clearly. Follow the tree from the roots of the trunk at the bottom to the sprouting branches and to its crest. Imagine details such as the bigger and smaller branches, whether there are leaves on the branches and what colour they are.

Now that you can see the tree in its entirety, imagine how the tree's roots spread out into the earth beneath it. How they anchor the tree and give it stability.

Experience how your own feet anchor you to the ground, as if roots were growing from your feet into that same soil.

Note the tree branches as if you were looking at them from beneath. See how they move in the wind. As if your body can be simultaneously relaxed and grounded. See a vertical line between the soil and the sky: Tied down and securely rooted, but also stretching upwards.

See the tree through different seasons, through the perspective of change: The changes in colour, how the leaves die and fall to the ground. And how new, bright green leaves grow back. As if something you have been carrying leaves you and something new comes of it.

See the tree through changes in the weather. Cool, strong winds come and tug at it, making the branches sway. But the roots keep the tree anchored in the soil and it stands firm in spite of everything. The wind dies down and becomes warm. Everything shifts and perhaps you can experience the same thing with your existence and feel that the variations and shifts are natural.

Hold this image of the tree in relation to your own body.

Your breathing is still a secure presence.

Stay still for a while while maintaining the feeling of being grounded.

Perhaps you can start to see trees in your daily life. Slow down and notice trees in your surroundings. Perhaps take a diversion through the park and think about the fact that they are breathing out oxygen for you, while you breathe out carbon dioxide for them.

III.

Meditation

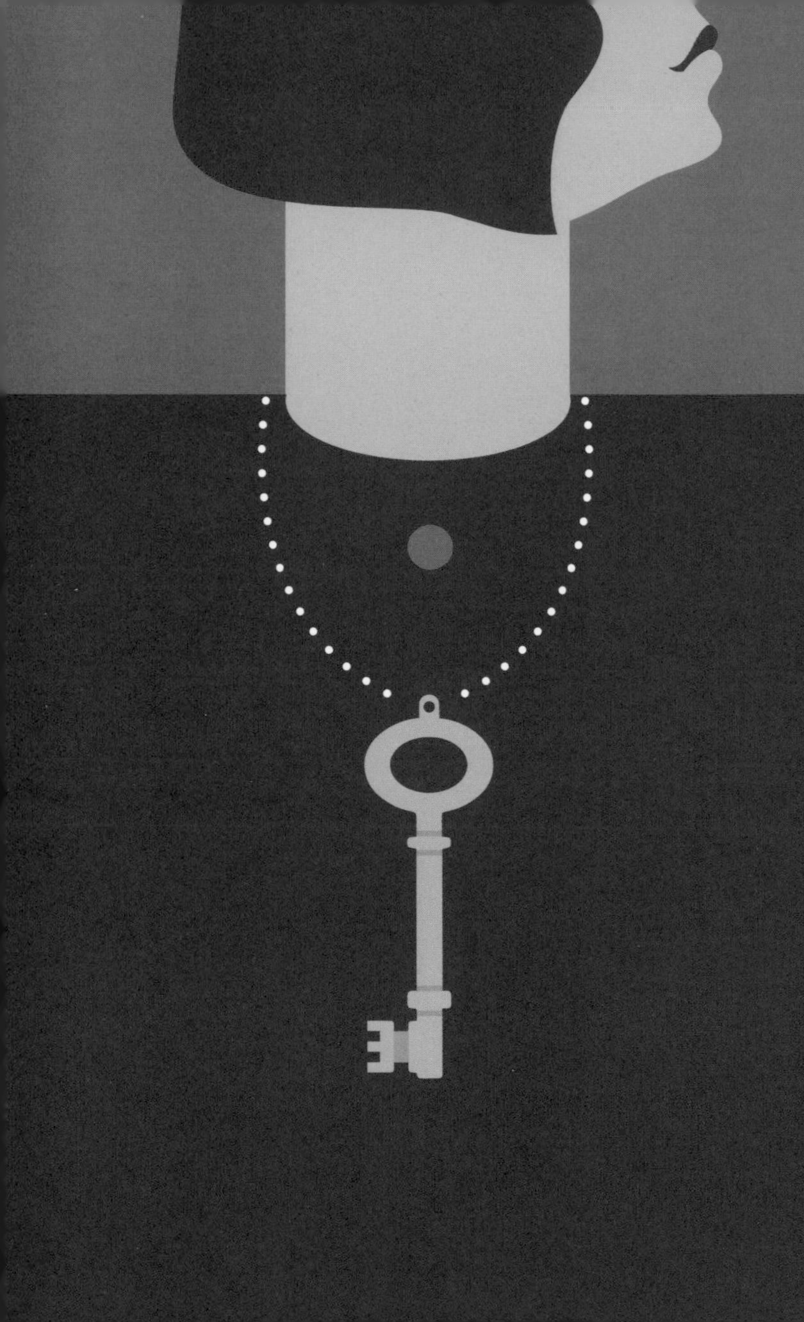

An Invisible Key

I learned to meditate when I was a teenager. Restlessness and anxiety often determined the conditions of my existence and I was very poor at being slow and reflective. Sometimes I would think to myself: Is this how it's supposed to be?

I couldn't maintain my concentration for very long unless it related to something I thought was especially interesting. At times I would discover glowing intensity. That would take me a long way, but all too often it was a struggle to maintain my concentration when the school teacher was reading aloud from a book and then asking questions about what they had just read. More often than not, I would lose focus. I don't know whether you can relate to the feeling of reading a book and finding that you have to read the same piece of text over and over again because you've forgotten what you've just read. In other words, you wouldn't have put your money on me being the next Olympic champion of meditation.

By chance, I became acquainted with Buddhism and I learned the art of meditation. A couple of different experiences – in themselves not that remarkable –

offering a hint of the bewitching power of meditation became crucial to my teenage self. Since then, it often feels like I have an invisible key hanging around my neck. A key that I can use at any time to open a door into a place beyond the stress of daily life. I am often drawn in, losing myself, getting lost. One time it may be work, but another time it might be my social life that has me on the hook and forces me to deal with tasks I would not have imagined would come my way. But the invisible key of meditation is within reach. With persistent practise over many years, it has been enriched with unadulterated force and the key continues to fit in the lock to allow me into one of the most beautiful rooms I have ever entered.

Meditation is – in a liberating way – a simple and effortless exercise that we can use to better understand our inner selves and our relationship with the outside world. Meditation is a big concept and can relate equally to better cultivating someone's inherent good qualities and not clinging on too tightly to things that don't have lasting value – or being so still that you are disarmed of all the burdens you have been carrying. When we get closer to our core, we can clearly experience whether a relationship needs repairing, better appreciate the life we have and even feel greater understanding of and affinity with the people around us.

Dudjom Rinpoche, a well-known Tibetan master of meditation, describes a meditative state that I recognise in myself: 'Imagine a person who returns home from a long day's work in the fields and sits down in their favourite armchair in front of a warm fire. He knows he has done a good job and there is nothing else to worry about. He can treat himself by staying in the state of being and leaving aside the doing.'

For someone like me in my younger years, who had never before experienced the deep stillness, this is truly a blessing.

It is like when a flickering candle flame is stabilised. Meditation settles the air around you. The flame rises and burns clearly.

When your mind becomes such a flame, your thoughts are permitted to slow down and an interface between stimuli and responses is opened up. When this happens, recovery is possible and you can induce deep rest between feelings and thoughts that would normally be difficult to manage. When the relaxation of your body provides resonance and merges with the mind – and interaction occurs between the two – something beautiful happens; the meditation begins to take shape in your body and in your daily life. I hope that this chapter will help contribute towards that.

139
Check-in

MEDITATION IS IMMEDIATELY restful for some people, while for others it is provocatively restless. It is important to understand and take this into account when considering it.

If you have been doing the exercises described in this book as you go along, you will probably have noticed that your mind – unlike your body – cannot easily be made still. It can take many different shapes over a short period of time: Anxious, restless, whimsical, imaginative, confused. But perhaps most of all, it can be uncontrollable – in this context it is similar to taming a wild horse, getting a hyperactive monkey to sit down or getting a drunken elephant to sober up.

Realising that your mind is like this is also a step forward in your progress. We understand that in the beginning there is a fragile boundary between presence and absence.

If you never get to be in silence during any form of presence training, perhaps it is an insight that you will have to continue living unaware of it. What is absent often tends to take up an unnecessary amount of space instead of giving us tools to work with.

A first exercise that can illustrate this may be simply to experience these movements and meanderings in relation to a presence.

Checking in is a tactile meditation exercise in which we can use an open mind to learn about how we function, where we are most situated during thought, how it impacts us and how we bring our mind back home again.

Sometimes we time travel into our future – *creating plans, preparing, experiencing before the experience happens, looking forward to it, or worrying.*

Other times, we move back into the past – *enjoying beautiful memories, writing about and justifying events, feeling grateful for something we were a part of, mourning the passing of time.*

Absurdly enough, what is harder to capture is the moment that we are actually in.

You can sit or lie down. Then rest the palms of your hands against your legs. Maintain a relaxed and vacant focus on your natural breathing and try to follow each tiny movement in the breathing cycle. For example, how your stomach moves when each inhalation and exhalation takes place.

If you notice that your mind is running away from you to thoughts of the past – ponderings, specific events in your history, funny memories – tap your fingertips gently on your *left* leg. This will bring you back to your focus on breathing.

On the other hand, if you notice your thoughts wandering off into the future – things that haven't yet happened, worry, disaster scenarios, fantasies – tap your fingertips gently on your *right* leg. This will bring you back to your focus on the present moment.

When other thoughts that don't touch upon either the past or future cross your mind and distract your focus, silently whisper the word *thought* in order to stop your thoughts from meandering away.

Each tap helps you to bring your focus back to your breathing, and teaches you about where you most often go when you are not in the present moment.

Don't be downhearted or surprised if you end up tapping your legs a lot to begin with.

Be kind to yourself – we're just practising.

143

Somewhere Else

IN THE MIDDLE of the conversation, one of my daughters exclaims in admonishment: 'You're not listening to me! You're somewhere else.'

Somewhere else. Yes, that's probably right. But where?

Often, we think about something completely different from what is happening around us in the moment that it is actually happening. As you will have noticed in the previous exercise, we often travel in our thoughts – and even though we try to focus, we will reel off in different directions, from trivialities to what is more important, in a happy blend of the two.

A thousand years ago, the Buddha used the *Dhammapada* sayings to tell his disciple Sangharakkhita: 'The mind may wander and think of things that have not yet happened. The best thing to do is to concentrate on the present and strive to free oneself from greed, hatred and hostility.'

In modern times, psychologists at Harvard University have concluded that 'a human mind is a wandering mind, and a wandering mind is an unhappy mind.' In this same study, they asked 2,250 participants aged 18–88 to answer a series of questions at randomly selected times of day.

The questions they were asked were about what the participants were doing at that moment, whether they were thinking about the task they were performing at the time, or whether they were thinking about something else pleasant, unpleasant or neutral.

The results showed that 46.9 per cent were thinking about something other than what they were actually doing during their waking hours. The same scenario was pervasive in most activities, such as shopping, watching TV, eating or walking. In correlation with the other questions posed and the time-shift analyses, it was possible to discern that participants were less happy in those time spans where they were not present. In this way, the amount of time our mind 'checks out' more clearly predicts how happy we are than what we are actually doing, and the volume of thoughts that are 'somewhere else' dominate our mental lives and health. The researchers commented after the fact that the results were in line with what several philosophical traditions had long since taught:

A wandering mind is an unhappy mind.

I remember where I first heard that.

ཨོཾ་མ་ཎི་པདྨེ་ཧཱུྃ

147

Mantra – a Substitute for all Thoughts

MANTRA, A SILENT or vocalised recitation of one or more words repeated, is both a substitute for the constant flow of thoughts and also a way of remaining in silence. The syllables of the mantra become a replacement for distracting thoughts and reduce their dominance over your mind. It is a beautiful and dynamic meditation, in which the words form a protective membrane around you and whisk you onto the path of silence. The ties between the words become looser, the distance between the syllables extends and the silence emerges.

As if a brake is applied or a switch turned off, activity ceases and wordlessly you come to a halt in an enveloping, dense silence. Eventually, the silence has replaced the flow of thoughts.

Simply appreciate it and remain there. When you express words, use your feeling for rhythm and music – don't become mechanical, instead let the words float.

One of the most common mantras in the Buddhist world

is *Om mani padme hum*. In the Buddhist context, this mantra is believed to waken and develop the latent compassion that is found in every human being. It is a lively mantra and when I recently visited Nepal, I was able to experience it being mumbled, uttered, even shouted during the walking meditation that many perform in the vicinity of the Buddhist buildings known as stupas. There is a well-conceived articulation in the six syllables of the mantra, and a direct translation of the mantra offers no decisive meaning – but finding the rhythm in the mantra and expressing it can be an invaluable pillar in meditation.

Another mantra that is more familiar to practitioners of yoga but with clear traits of the message of compassion is *Lokah Samastah Sukhino Bhavantu*. The translation from Sanskrit reads: *May all beings everywhere be happy and free*.

Put your hands together in front of your chest and say it to yourself, and reflect on its meaning. Direct it at yourself, those who are nearby and everyone else who is alive.

If you prefer to use words spoken in your own language, here is a mantra that – with its responsive sonority – will do very well.

When you breathe in, silently say *inhalation*. When you breathe out, silently say *exhalation*. At the end of your exhalation and in the pause before your next inhalation, silently say *stillness*.

151

Adversity as a Friend

WHEN I ASK the people to whom I teach meditation what the hardest part of meditation is, the answer is usually the tormenting feeling of restlessness, the divisive thoughts and the downward spiralling negative feelings. I can relate to these, and there is no reason to deny to ourselves that it is hard to go from a hyper-connected world to stillness.

Hopefully, we have already acquired enough good experiences of meditation to think it is worth continuing, and that means we also need tools to use in adversity, during the actual moment of meditation and in the various stages of life itself.

With a particular attitude to our experiences that is characterised by openness, curiosity and acceptance, we seem – in these moments – more easily able to accommodate what happens in our inner selves. Acceptance is not just a highly effective attitude that provides the individual with a more open, flexible perspective that can help an agitated mind to transition to a calmer state.

Meditation also involves an acceptance in the sense that we cannot simply expect to experience certain emotional states in meditation while other less welcome ones disappear. Instead, we let things be without controlling, intervening or correcting.

Meditation carried out without acceptance is like a boxer fighting his shadow with no hope of victory. A wiser attitude is to see all mental activity as the same: Clouds on the sky that appear from nowhere and disappear after a while.

When meditating in stillness, you can focus on the intervals between your thoughts and mental images, but an even more effective approach is to look at what is disturbing you with a clarity of presence. For example, if you start thinking about something that triggers stress or anxiety, interrupt the thought by silently naming the thought according to its content. This might be work, family, trivialities, etc. By stamping the thought this way, you avoid blocking it, but you simultaneously gently push it away by seeing it and accepting it. More often than not, the adversity is soon forgotten.

Let me explain acceptance and a direct view of the obstacles to it, by recounting a story about the Tibetan yogi Milarepa and how he escaped his own demons by inviting them to tea. Milerepa is a well-known figure in Tibetan literature, and his journey from murderous to enlightened is one of the most popular in Tibetan literary history. For only in confronting his own actions could he be liberated.

One evening, Milerepa is strolling home to his cave. He is clutching firewood to his thin body. When he steps into his dwelling, he discovers he has visitors: His demons. In the brief time he has been away, they have made themselves at home, started eating his food, reading his books and even sleeping in his bed. Even though he recognises this is only happening in his head – he is face-to-face with the least desirable traits within himself – he has no idea how to get the demons to leave the cave. At first, he simply wants to throw them out, one by one, from the cave. But after a while, Milarepa comes to his senses and deals with the demons with compassion. Initially, none of his visitors take any notice but just try to disturb him. Milarepa loses patience, but when he raises his voice to order them to leave, he is met with nothing but scornful laughter.

Milarepa sits down on the hard, stone floor. Meeting their gazes, he calmly explains: 'Since neither you nor I intend to leave, we'll have to live here together. You're most welcome; we share everything.' As soon as he said that, the demons vanished.

Meditation in Movement

AROUND 10 YEARS ago, I learned the form of yoga known as ashtanga yoga. This happened during a period where sleep had become a rarity, I was completely stressed and daily life felt like a long struggle that would hopefully come to an end someday.

Meditation had long helped me in many ways, but since my body felt weak, stiff and immovable, I desperately needed physical activity. I had regular experiences of pain and loss of feeling in my physical body, but there was also deep, underlying emotional pain. The county council's emergency therapy and rehabilitation service generously offered me support, but at this time it only had a slight effect.

My single-mindedness had taken me back and forth to India and Nepal countless times, and it had focused on the details of Tibetan Buddhism, but it had never once noticed that I was in the middle of yoga's home region. Instead, I was sitting in our apartment searching online to find a yoga studio that best matched the few gaps in my calendar and that wasn't too far from my home.

In my search, I found a number of video clips from the early 80s demonstrating the yoga form I would later fall for. There was an immediate appeal that instantly captured my imagination. There was a clearly thought-through framework, which suited me, and even though I was in very poor shape, I could absorb the clear and concise instructions issued: *Breathe in, raise your arms up, breathe out, bend forward... Breathe in, bend back*, and so on.

Sometime later, I heard a teacher in an altogether positive context describe ashtanga yoga as a *caveman practice*. I understood exactly what they meant: *Raise your arms* – and I raised, and once I had done so I could also shakily bend forward.

I had missed a couple of sessions at the beginning of the course, which meant I was thrown straight into an intense, high tempo, guided sequence. The schedule of movements appeared obvious to the other participants, and I did my best to follow. In those positions where I was bending forward, my legs shook like leaves even though I was doing literally everything I could to keep them still. I breathed irregularly and sweat began to pour after just a few minutes, dripping onto the yoga mat. The directions left and right suddenly no longer seemed quite so obvious, and at times I had no idea which way I was meant to turn. I remember experiencing it all as somewhat troubling and my own self-image was tarnished – after all, I was a practised meditator. I stumbled from position to position, and it is impossible to use words such as 'smooth' or 'gracious' in this context.

The final standing position in the first series of ashtanga yoga is called *Virabadrasana*, somewhat carelessly translated as 'the warrior position'. In short, it involves setting one leg at 90 degrees to the other, with your foot pointing at the front edge of the yoga mat. Your other leg is stretched backwards and your upper body is balanced steadily in the middle. Your arms are fully extended in an exact horizontal line and your head is turned so that you can look forward at the hand that is in line with the bent knee. When you do it right, you look strong, graceful and almost as if you have stopped in the middle of a movement.

It's a beautiful position that radiates balance, strength and integrity.

Right there, at a moment when I was close to giving up, something that was incredible from my perspective happened. It was as if something joined together – a kind of complete assimilation between body and breathing. A maximum presence spread all the way from right down in my toes up through my legs and then up my spine. Suddenly, calm radiated through my head. My body felt light and everything in that moment was in absolute equilibrium. As the philosopher Patanjali describes the phenomenon in the eternally relevant text *Yoga Sutras*, dating from 500 years ago:

'An asana, a body position is mastered through lowering effort and meditating upon the infinite. Thus, we are undisturbed by the dualities of life.'

When I opened my eyes after that in the final phase of lying and resting that is mandatory in yoga, there lingered a feeling of completeness throughout my entire body. Several years of burden had been lifted from my shoulders, things that had been separated were slowly put back together again, a feeling I hadn't felt in a long time. What had been broken felt in that moment to have been fixed.

Shortly after, I made a decision. An important decision about a new structure to my daily life featuring yoga six days a week. Six days because that is how the tradition of ashtanga yoga is practised.

A decision I stand firmly by, more than 10 years later. Now I know how movement can lead to stillness, as well as how stillness functions in movement.

In the precise joining of breathing and movement, it turned out the wonderful was to be found.

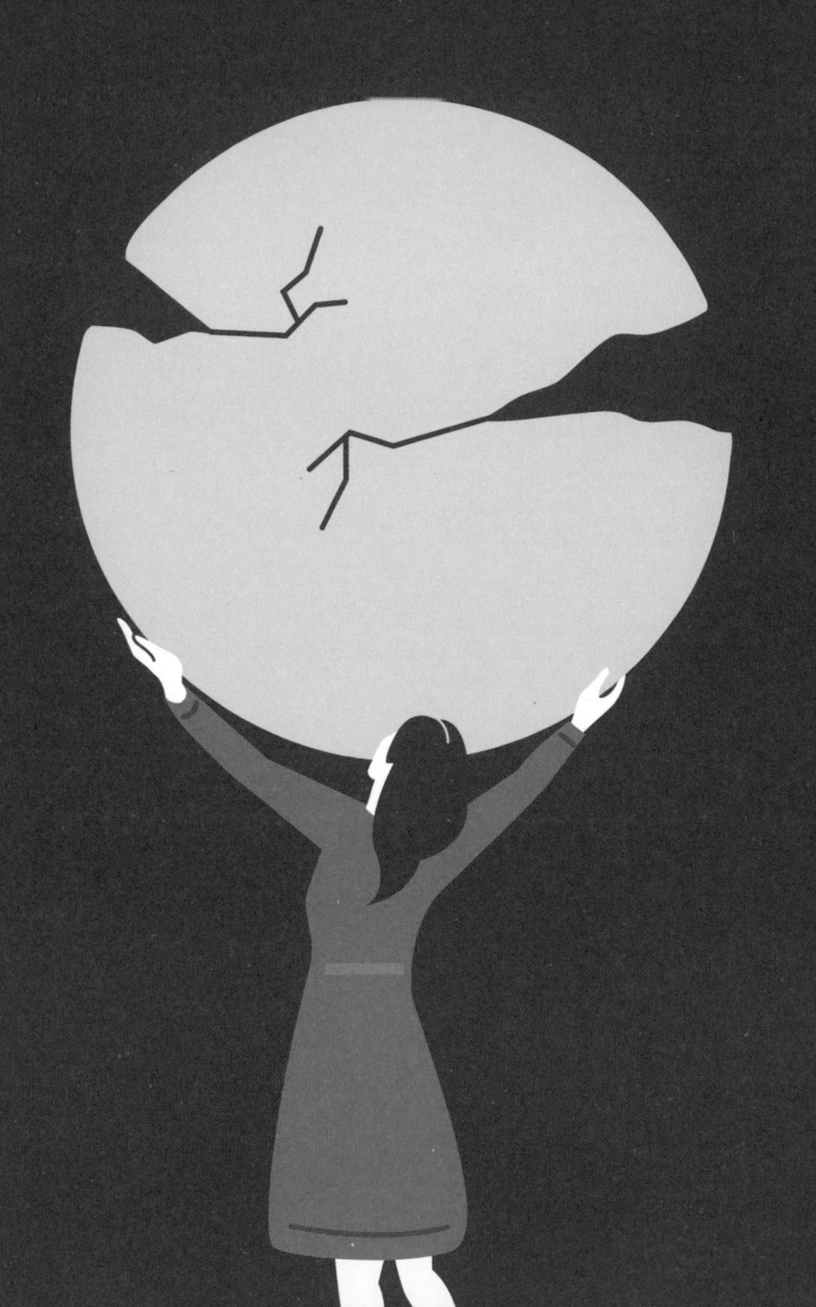

161
Meditation Beyond Pain

AS PART OF my writing process, I want to broaden my view, to gain more perspectives on what meditation can be and mean on an individual level. I arrange to meet my friend Josefine Bengtsson at Il Caffè on Drottninggatan in central Stockholm. It's a Monday afternoon. Cloaked in the grey of November. The darkness coalesces and I walk up the hill towards the Tegnérlunden park, twisting my head at all angles so that I can read the words of August Strindberg: 'To love is to give: Give!' etched in the asphalt.

Josefine has been a well-known yoga teacher for many years, working all over the world, leading popular yoga practices with gusto. Many young people on the verge of burnout come to her to participate in retreats that explore dynamic forms of meditation and long periods of silence. She speaks sincerely about how particular she is in creating a safe space for participants, where they have the opportunity to rediscover something inside themselves that seems to have been lost in the crazy tempo of modern life. Many people are like the person she once was, at the time when she switched from being a diligent student at the Stockholm School of Economics to a career as a strategic consultant: 'I had claustrophobia in my own body. I said I was going out running, but in practice I went running because I needed the moment that I reached after total exhaustion. That was the only time when I could feel relaxed. When my body stopped, I experienced stillness I could no longer feel in my daily life.'

She describes the rising interest in participating in retreats like hers. More and more people – bordering on burnt-out but still maintaining a pace that they simply can't stop – come to her with a desire for stillness. She explains that upon arrival, many are stressed almost to breaking point – worried and anxious. It is often the case that to begin with, their focus is excessively on the outer. A habit of being in control in order to manage external stresses, in which things like what different foods contain or some other external detail can become big deals.

Josefine continues: 'We love control, but what makes us feel alive is when we lose control. When you let go, something you may not have done since you were little, something happens. You find the way into your heart: The essence of your self. The tears usually come after a few days as a result of a range of strong emotions.

That's necessary, because after that the self-love returns. Many people describe it as... forgiving themselves.'

As we talk, it occurs to me how little I know about Josefine, even though we are friends.

Every time we meet, we talk about the passion we share for matters pertaining to the contemplative spectrum. I listen, recognise myself and learn.

Our order arrives. We keep it simple – hot water with ginger – and talk about scaling back and through simplification finding the way to the core. Josefine calls it 'the essence', while I use phrases like 'innermost stillness'. The more I listen, the more I understand that, small differences aside, we mean the same thing – and just as is the case for me, the alchemy of meditation has released a source of friction.

'I now know that there was a pain that I had fled earlier in my life. During the school holidays, it was always so clearly present and that scared me. It felt good when the summer holidays ended, because then I could push it away by being busy again. When I was alone, I always kept myself active and moving. If I was at the gym, I would have my school books with me and do several things at once. I ran and ran to avoid confronting the pain. Everyone is so scared of it, but now I'm friends with it and my experience is that there is always something beautiful behind that pain. I've always felt that. When I stopped running and stayed in what hurt, there was only presence left. When I get there, I feel connected to everything and I feel that there is a connection with others. I feel like I'm part of something big.'

The paths to stillness can differ, but they lead to the same point. For me, meditation fell into my lap in my youth, while for Josefine it involved an inevitable decision to completely leave behind the professional career she had invested in, in order to follow a new way. She explains that it came at a high cost, with the world around not always being able to accept her choice.

Such a choice requires great courage, as the meditation master Chögyam Trungpa breathtakingly puts it: 'The bad news is you're falling through the air, nothing to hang on to, no parachute. The good news is, there's no ground.'

167

Being Kind to Yourself and Others

THERE IS A long list of the known effects of meditation on people: Lower cortisol levels, fewer feelings of worry, less anxiety, improved ability to focus, better sleep, enhanced memory and emotional competence. But the most beautiful thing that meditation can create is the ability to evoke the innermost good in a person. It is not only a core value, but the method that in a number of studies has achieved the highest levels of happiness. Meditation on compassion can cause us to overcome self-centring that all too often becomes expressed in our lives. When this happens, our perspective slowly moves away from the desire to win, from jealously guarding your preserves of friendship with yourself and your inadequacies, as well as with others and their shortcomings.

This is both the foundation and the goal at the same time. Being compassionate and loving is possible for the individual in solitary meditation, and as a commitment in daily life. Through a gradual process of endowing your own mind with good and cultivating compassion towards your surroundings. As Simone

Weil so beautifully describes it, in the depths of every human heart from earliest childhood until the grave, there is 'something, which, despite all the hurt we have caused, suffered and witnessed, unquestionably expects us to show kindness and not add hurt. This is above all else the thing that is sacred to every human being. The good is the only source of the sacred. Nothing is sacred except the good, and what is associated with the good.'

I have often heard that kindness is connected with lower intelligence. But kindness, goodness and care don't just create better mental health. There are a number of interesting studies that show that kindness and the willingness to understand others create the psychological security in a group that leads to better results. Those who dare to share ideas and their knowledge, and are less jealously guarding of their preserves get more back than those who do the opposite. Generosity and encouragement, as well as giving others space and glory, is a more certain way to secure common progress.

Find out what the impact is like in your direct surroundings: Try expressing your appreciation of those around you or to someone who you happen to bump into in daily life. We all know how an unexpected but friendly conversation with a stranger can affect us. How excited we feel at a little consideration from an unknown person. That wonderful feeling of context. The feeling of being a part.

Perhaps it has its origins in being able to be kind and loving to yourself. Strangely enough, it doesn't always seem to be that simple. Let's try. Perhaps this is an exercise you can start your day with.

Stand in front of a mirror and look yourself in the eyes and say: 'I'm doing the best I can. I am good enough and I am worthy of the very best. I am worthy to love and to be loved.' Say this tentatively a couple of times and then let it come from your heart more naturally. If it is too hard, close your eyes and put one hand gently on your heart and say it out loud. Once you can direct the words at yourself and properly take them in, it becomes easier to wish for the same fundamental rights for others.

As a final exercise, I want to share a meditation that has followed me through the years. I learned it long ago on one of my first visits to Nepal.

In the exercise, we break in and stop the negative dominoes from falling; we replace the darkness with a lighter self-image. We gradually let go of our old mistakes, problems that have etched themselves in and trapped us. We put down our burdens, let confidence settle in and hopefully we make peace with ourselves.

Use what you have learned so far from the book. How you sit or lie, how you first relax your body and then make yourself present with your own breathing, how you find still focus and let the noise of your thoughts move into the background.

Create an intention for your meditation. Remember that you're not just doing the meditation exercise for yourself, but as a kind act for everyone around you – no exceptions.

Direct an increasingly precise focus on your breathing. Each time you breathe out, imagine everything weighing you down, everything that seems like an unwanted burden, leaving your body in the form of black smoke. Follow it out of the room and imagine it dissolving. Experience lightness in your body once it has completely left you.

Repeat for a moment in stillness so that it feels natural. Experience how stress, strong emotions, ponderings, all worries and anxiety are forgotten.

Then, when you breathe in through your nose, imagine how you are breathing in something new – what is good, and what you want more of – in the form of a white light. The light spreads throughout all parts of your body, filling every cell, and making you feel light and relaxed.

Experience for a continuous moment of stillness how the heaviness within you leaves your body when you breathe out, and how the liberating lightness reaches into you when you breathe in. Before ending your meditation, place your hands back together in front of your chest, touch the skin of the fingers of each hand gently together and wish everyone around you well-being, love and stillness in their lives.

173

The Easy and the Difficult

A FEW YEARS ago, I led a meditation on a Barcelona rooftop, and afterwards I asked those attending how they had found the period of meditation. An afternoon breeze cooled us in the blazing sun and a woman explained how her whole presence had rested on how the gentle breeze had touched her hair. So let your search for stillness be a beautiful experience. See it wherever you go. How stillness conceals itself in every moment given to you in life.

Meditation is simplicity and difficulty. So always treat yourself with humility. There are always those people who know everything, who have understood everything and want to have the final word. Just let them be and focus on practise. On your own experience. That's what you keep and what eventually makes a real difference.

In the introduction to this book, I described my daily meditation as an almost powerfully still moment. 'Regardless of mood or circumstance, a happiness that knows no bounds.'

So it is and nothing else has taught me in the same way how to stabilise a restless and anxious mind, illuminated my path and taught me to remain relaxed about things outside my control. Meditation is the path to nothing that also fills your inner self to the brim with something. Something that gives everything meaning.

Last of all, let us sit in silence for a while, before you close the cover of this book and we part ways.

Sit with gratitude in your heart. To yourself and others.

For the life given to you.

A point of stillness. Even if the world around you remains noisy.

References

THE ART OF STILLNESS IN A NOISY WORLD

Pascal, Blaise (2006), *Pensées* [Thoughts], Ökade insatser mot psykisk ohälsa på grund av jobbet' [Increased efforts against poor mental health due to work], Swedish Work Environment Authority, 19/02/2019, https://www.av.se/press/okade-insatser-mot-psykisk-ohalsa-pa-grund-av-jobbet/

STILLNESS IS EVERYTHING AND NOTHING

Dagerman, Stig (1947), *Nattens lekar* [The Games of Night], Norstedts förlag

THE STILLNESS WE SEEK

Gansten, Martin; Broo, Måns (2005), *De tidiga upanisaderna* [The Early Upanishads], Bokförlaget Nya Doxa

Björling, Gunnar (1957), *Du jord du dag: Urval lyrik* [You Earth, You Day: Selected Poems], Wahlström & Widstrand

THE ART OF DOING NOTHING

Seneca, (2013), *Om livets korthet* [On the Shortness of Life], Bokförlaget Daidalos

MINDFULNESS IN DAILY LIFE

Sifferlin, Alexandra (2015), 'Washing Dishes Is a Really Great Stress Reliever, Science Says' http://time.com/4056280/ washing-dishes-stress-relief-mindfulness/, 30/09/2015

BREATHING SPACE

LaMotte, Sandee (2017), 'Hillary Clinton uses alternate-nostril breathing. Should you?' https://edition.cnn.com/2017/09/14/health/hillary-clinton-alternate-nostril-breathing/index.html

FEELING COMFORT IN CHANGE

Merton, Thomas (2012), *The Inner Experience: Notes on Contemplation*, HarperCollins

Konnikova, Maria (2014), 'The Lost Art of the Unsent Angry Letter', *The New York Times*, 22/03/2014

CHANGES IN DAILY LIFE

Center for Humane Technology, App Ratings http://humanetech.com

Burkus, David (2014), 'The Creative Benefits of Boredom', *Harvard Business Review*, 09/09/2014

BEING AT ONE WITH LISTENING

Chozen Bays, Jan (2011), *How to Train a Wild Elephant: And Other Adventures in Mindfulness*, Shambala

A TREE IN MY GARDEN

Lagerkvist, Elin (1963), *Zen: en Zenbuddhistisk antologi* [Zen: a Zen Buddhist Anthology], Natur och Kultur

Cowper Powys, John (1930), *The Meaning of Culture*, London: Jonathan Cape

'Green spaces deliver lasting mental health benefits' (2014), Science Daily http://www.exeter.ac.uk/news/featurednews/title_349054_en.html 07/01/2014

Popkin, Gabriel (2017), 'Nature videos help to calm inmates in solitary confinement', *Nature*, 01/09/2017

Kardan, Omid; Gozdyra, Peter; et al. (2015) 'Neighborhood greenspace and health in a large urban center', *Scientific Reports 5* Article number 11610

THE FIXED POINT

Singh, Anita, 'Voice of the shipping forecast returns to lull listeners to sleep – but not on the BBC', *The Telegraph*, 29/03/2017

'Sjörapporten – därför behöver vi den' [The Shipping Forecast – Why We Need It], Vetenskapsradion, Sveriges Radio, https://sverigesradio.se/sida/artikel.aspx?programid=406&artikel=6967820 8.6.2018

THE GHOST PARK

Ekström, Hjalmar (2007), *Utblottelse: ett urval betraktelser ur Det fördolda lifvet av Hjalmar Ekström och andra kristna mystiker* [Missing out: a selection of considerations from The Hidden Life of Hjalmar Ekström and other Christian mystics], Eolit Förlag

TOWARDS SILENCE

Matthiessen, Peter (1978), *The Snow Leopard*, Viking Press

Dahl, Roald (1977) *The Wonderful Story of Henry Sugar and Six More*, Random House

IN SILENCE

Stafford, William (1999), *The Way It Is: New and Selected Poems*, Graywolf Press

THE GREATEST POSSIBLE SILENCE

Picard, Max (1988), *The World of Silence*, Gateway Editions

Björling, Gunnar (1995), *Skrifter I–V* [Writings I-V], Erikssons förlag

Lubow, Arthur (2010), 'The Sound of Spirit', *The New York Times*, 15/10/2010.

AN INVISIBLE KEY

'Dudjom Rinpoche about Meditation 1979' https://www.youtube.com/watch?v=qbJ7u_nJb54

Bakewell, Sarah (2010), 'Montaigne, philosopher of life, part 4: Borrowing the cat's point of view', *The Guardian*, 31/05/2010

SOMEWHERE ELSE

Bradt, Steve (2010), 'Wandering mind not a happy mind', The Harvard Gazette, https://news. harvard.edu/gazette/story/2010/11/ wandering-mind-not-a-happy-mind/, 11/11/2010

MEDITATION IN MOVEMENT

Satchidananda, Swami (2012), *The Yoga Sutras of Patanjali,* Integral Yoga Publications

BEING KIND TO YOURSELF AND OTHERS

Weil, Simone (1961), *La personne et le sacré* [The Person and the Holy], Bonnier